Contents

Preface

Some years ago it was suggested that I write a book about my life. The reason being it might be of help to others. While I appreciated the suggestion, I was not the least bit interested in telling my story. Previous to this time it had also been suggested by a few people that I publish my poetry. I had no interest in doing that either. I was content to read one of my poems when it fit an occasion and content also to leave both my story and poetry publicly untold.

In April, 2017, something changed in me and a desire sprung forth to write this book. My hope is that you will find encouragement in these pages and then be brave and humble enough to blow the trumpet as the need arises.

"'When you go to war in your land against the enemy who oppresses you, then you shall sound an alarm with the trumpets, and you will be remembered before the Lord your God, and you will be saved from your enemies' (New King James Version, Num. 10.9)."

I've used the word "enemy" here as any trial, test, weight, or situation in which you need a brother or sister with whom to share your load. Recently this verse jumped out at me and I knew Blow the Trumpet was the title I wanted my book to be.

In the preface of a book the writer is to be able to establish his or her credibility and experience that pertains to the topic. My experience and credibility are that I lived this life.

Dedication

How does one decide to whom to dedicate a book when the book encompasses one's whole life, and when that life has been influenced and surrounded by myriads of people? I find this a daunting task. Many people contributed to my life's walk and I know there are many of you who will not see your name here. I ask for your understanding and know that no manner of slight has been intended.

I dedicate this book...

- In memory of my father and mother, Robert and Dorothy Coldren, who were faithful and loving parents; I am privileged to have been their daughter.
- In honor of my children, Melody Lynn Patrick and Jeffrey Adam Leaman, Sr. They walked most of my life with me, and from them I have experienced love and forgiveness, and the beautiful privilege of watching their on-going growth. I thank the Lord for them. There are not adequate words to express the love and respect I feel for them.
- In appreciation to my daughter, Melody, for her artwork on the cover. She inherited her artistic ability from her Great-grandmother Zarfoss.
- In honor of the friends who walked by my side through the hard years: Joanne, Sue, and Cherl. Thank you for the shoulders you let me cry on.
- In memory of Jack, a Christian counselor who did his best to guide me, and taught me how to listen to the heart cry of others; also in appreciation to Bonnie, another Christian counselor who picked up where Jack left off, and who remains a friend to this day. The Lord used both these people to encourage and support me.
- In honor of Joyce who took the time to read and make necessary grammatical corrections to this book. I value your friendship.

- With a thankful heart and appreciation to my son Jef, who did extensive work to ready this manuscript in order for it to be sent on its way for whatever purpose God has.
- With reverence, awe, and gratefulness I dedicate this book to my Savior, Jesus Christ for His forgiveness, encouragement, and hope; I dedicate this book to the Holy Spirit whose voice and guidance I value; and to Almighty God whose ways and wisdom are beyond human comprehension. Thank you for the privilege of writing this book, and for graciously giving me life. My prayer and hope is that it will complete the purpose You have for it.

Introduction

What you will be reading in this book is a collection of poems and songs that I wrote beginning at age 15. You will see things composed during some very dark times in my life. You may sometimes wonder at the questions I asked, and the feelings I experienced. You will be given insight as to what was going on at the time of each writing. You will read of the struggles that many families experience, ours in particular. You will see into the deepest recesses of my heart, as I knew it; but I want to make it clear that only God really knows what is in a person's heart.

You will also read portions of God's Holy Word, and witness His never-ending faithfulness. You will notice that I used different versions of the Bible during my devotional time. I mean no disrespect to God's word. I generally prefer the King James Version and New King James Version, and believe them to be the most accurate. Though there were times in my life I read from the Amplified, the Living New Testament and the New International Version. The Lord will not be told how or when to speak to a person's heart; He is not hindered by which version of His word we are reading.

Here we go!
Take a walk with me, my friends;
Up the mountains, and down again;
Through the desert, and into the sea;
Down in the valley, take a walk with me.

What is the definition of "walk"? Merriam-Webster includes the following in its definition: "to move with your legs at a speed that is slower than running. [2]"

Synonyms offered by Thesaurus.com include saunter, hike, tread, stroll, traipse, jaunt, step, gait, promenade [4] (and various others).

In the poetry I've written I have used seven of the above words, and in my walk of life, I have used the majority. Probably you have also.

This book is about my life. It is not easy to write, nor will all of it be an easy read. My life was, and will continue to be a life of challenge, hope, and victory. We are each born to experience these.

Many good and wonderful times are part of my life; many good and loving people, as well.

There have also been those times in life when I've felt hopeless, stuck, and defeated. But praise God, He brought me up and out of those difficult seasons. It is never His desire that we live a hopeless, stuck and defeated life.

> "'To everything there is a season, a time for every matter or purpose under heaven' (Amplified, ' (King James Version, Eccles. 3.1)."

Very few of you who read this book know me; our paths will probably never cross. I am not famous, not even known, except perhaps to a few hundred people. I am neither rich nor poor, beautiful nor homely in the public's eye. I am not ignorant nor exceptionally intelligent. I am not self-effacing nor boastful. You could easily have lived beside me. We could have been neighbors. Possibly I am you.

This is a walk no one else has taken. You, walk your own walk. Your walk may be more difficult, or it may be a smoother one. There may be great differences in our walks, but you may find there are also a number of similarities, for we are all human. This is not a literal walking on two feet that I am speaking of, but rather a life walk which includes joy and sorrow, anguish of heart, soul, and mind; doubting, and faith. Sometimes I walked backwards for a bit; sometimes sideways (skirting the issues if you will), and many times straight forward; but always walking. I continue to walk, and Jesus walks with me. I do not always know where I am going. I just know He and I are walking together. He knows the way. Sometimes the walk is smooth and delightful; sometimes it is over thorny and difficult territory; sometimes it is exciting; always it requires a steadfast desire to keep going; one day at a time; one foot in front of the other.

"'Wherein ye greatly rejoice, though now for a season, if need be, ye are in heaviness through manifold temptations: that the trial of your faith, being much more precious than of gold that perisheth, though it be tried with fire, might be found unto praise and honour and glory at the appearing of Jesus Christ' (King James Version, 1 Pet. 1.6-7)."

"'But He knoweth the way that I take: when He hath tried me, I shall come forth as gold' (King James Version, Job 23.10)."

The mountains and valleys are fewer and further between now, but the treks in the desert still bear my emotional footprints, at least in the recesses of my mind, however I walk more on level ground. I still need the Lord to walk with me, for He continues to have things to teach me, and He still has things for me to do.

I have found on my walk that even in the desert, the Lord can furnish a table of food. It might be noted here that all food is not necessarily eaten by mouth; some of it is eaten with the mind, and some food is eaten with the heart. Rotten food, in any form, chewed, and digested in any way will cause the body to be sick. The same can be said of the rotten things we chew on in our minds. Those foods will bring disease to our spirit; our very souls may suffer as well. Believe me, I know. I have not always taken healthy food into my body, or my mind. So if you are walking now in a desert place, go daily to the "filling station" of God's word, and eat of it. You cannot go wrong by eating there.

My walk begins in 1940 when my parents married. My mother was 20, and my father was 21. They began dating at 16, and 17. They never dated anyone else. It was a lifelong love until my mother passed away shortly before their 40th anniversary. I was conceived two months after their marriage. I am blessed.

APRIL 24, 1941   I am born.   All life is given by God.

"'I will praise Thee; for I am fearfully and wonderfully made' (King James Version, Ps. 139.14)."

"'Thou art worthy, O Lord, to receive glory and
honour and power: for thou hast created all things,
and for thy pleasure they are and were created'
(King James Version, Rev. 4.11)."

That means you, and that means me. We were created by Him, and for
His purpose.

1
In the Beginning

In the late 1940s, as a little girl, I would sometimes pretend I was a librarian. I read books such as Mother Goose, Nancy Drew, and The Bobbsey Twins, to name a few. I would tape blank sheets of paper in each one of my books, with its title and the date, hoping someone would check it out (which of course, they never did), and the date of return, (which wasn't necessary); it doesn't take a great deal of thought to figure out why.

In the 1950s the local newspaper in York, Pennsylvania. ran a poetry column for young poets. If your poem was selected you would see it in print, along with your name, address, and a silver dollar. I was hoping for both! I sat down and composed the following poem about spring, and waited for the coveted results. Later in life I would come to recognize this ability to put feelings and thoughts into words on paper as a personal gift from God. He knew I would need it, and He knew He would use it. I had no idea what a valuable gift He gave me.

Is there a personal gift God has given you that you have not recognized, or unwilling, or afraid to use?

MAY, 1956   I am 15 years old. My goal was accomplished!

Spring
Out of the month of April we go,
Away from the winds and soft falling snow;
Into the month of May which brings
Robins and bluebirds - all sorts of nice things -

Gay daffodils and violets bright,
Beautiful sunshine to give us each light;
Remember the clouds, so lovely and sweet;
They bring us the rain beneath our feet.

The showers so pleasingly bright,
Sparkle in daytime, shine at night.
From grass, so green come flowers fair.
Look all around you! It's spring everywhere!

In 1953 I accepted Jesus as my Savior. I was 12. I was well-behaved, sensitive, and I felt things deeply. As I matured in my faith I recognized that it doesn't matter how good or bad we are, we each need The Savior, Jesus Christ. We are born sinners, but sweet as we are at birth, we are still born sinners, and need to come to Him, and accept the gift of salvation that He offers us. This is why He was born, and this is why He died. He is the only way to an eternal life with God, The Father.

We will each spend that eternity somewhere.

Don't miss the previous sentence; stop and think about it. Jesus is an extremely important Person in my life. I needed a relationship with Him when I was young, and I continue to need that relationship.

You either know you do, or you don't know you do, but you do.

As I reflect on my childhood I realize I was extremely idealistic, and a dreamer. I was protected, and guided, and I knew what was expected of me. The expectation was that I be good. And truly as good as a human being can be, I was good. I had good examples. The Bible describes it as a Godly heritage. I was very fortunate.

"'For Thou, O God, hast heard my vows; Thou hast
given me the heritage of those that fear Thy name'
(King James Version, Ps. 61.5)."

2

My Heritage

At this point I'd like to introduce you to some of my family members. Of my birth family only my brother and I are still living.

My Father

My father always sought to do things right, and think before acting. Though I never felt close to my him, I always knew him to be a very respectable man. He was a hard worker; a faithful husband; bright, introverted, and self-effacing. I remember sometimes he would refer to himself as a dummy when he would make a mistake. That always bothered me. It may have subtly suggested to me that making mistakes was cause for shame. He was also serious, but at times he would chase my brother and me around the dining room table, and we would squeal with delight until we were breathless. He was very proud of me, but I always believed it was because I was good.

My father was musical. He taught himself to play the piano, with a little help from his mother. He taught himself to play a guitar. He liked to dance, and sometimes he would dance with my mother, which was sweet. I seem to remember him dancing with me as I stood on his shoes. I guess that is what little girls used to do in the 1940s. My father was in the Army, and perhaps for that reason he was very organized, and precise about things. He was always on time, or more than likely, early. He was a sergeant in WWII. I remember him telling me a few years ago about some of his time in the service, and he made a statement that I will always remember. He said, "I never did anything I was ashamed of." I have no trouble believing that.

My father was also an excellent ball player; a left-handed batter, and second baseman. He was invited to join a major league when he was in the service, but that would have required a move to NY, and he turned it down because of my mother and me, his infant daughter. I never heard him complain about that decision. As my brother and I grew to grade school age he taught us how to "batter up", and hit a soft ball. He was also a champion marble player, and he showed us how to play marbles. I still remember the "knucklers". They were the big marbles used to start the game. Some of them were very colorful.

My father could draw, and when he was in the service he would send ink drawn pictures home to my brother and me of cartoon characters, or planes, telling us to be good. It must have been very hard for him to be away from all of us.

My father was a smoker when I was a child. I can remember him sending me to "Effie and Emmys" Grocery store, up the street from our house, to buy him Lucky Strikes. When he came to Jesus for salvation, he decided to stop smoking. Some 30 years later, he took to smoking a cigar. He never smoked the cigar in the house, but rather outside in his work shed. When my mother died, he blamed himself for her death from Lymphoma, because of all the smoking he did in his younger years. She never smoked. He felt he should have been the one to die rather than her. I never believed that to be true, but he felt so bad about it.

In the early years he worked on the railroad and in 1953 he was invited to bring his family to revival services by one of his railroad co-workers. It is ironic that this very same co-worker was a man who exposed himself to me when our family was visiting him and his wife. I was 12.

We each came to Jesus as a result of this invitation. My parents, my brother and I began our own walk with the Lord at this time. One thing I wish is that we would have shared more about our "walk" through the years.

My father died at age 89, a life well lived. I remember you as "daddy", "pop", (which my brother called him for a time), and "dad". I love you dad, and want to thank you for all the things you taught me. You were a good and faithful man. I have always been proud of you. I am glad you are with the Lord now, for when you saw Him "face to face", I'm sure you saw just how much He loved you. You knew while living here that He died for you, but to see it in His eyes would bring a new realization of your worth.

My Mother

My mother was kind. She liked lovely things, and always kept our home nice and neat; she taught me how to do the same. She was an excellent seamstress, like my grandmother, and made many of my dresses even into high school. I always proudly wore them. (She even made her own dress to wear in later years to my wedding, and a hat to go with it!) She had a nice sense of style. She attempted to teach me to sew, but it only put knots in my stomach. I can do it, I just don't particularly enjoy it. She also taught me how to crochet, knit, iron, cook, and mother. She never thought as highly of herself as others did. I don't know why. She was a very sincere, pretty, and intelligent woman. She was sensitive and pensive as well.

My mother was well liked, and was a thoughtful, fun, and creative hostess to those who came to our home. As in most families she was the one who arranged our social calendar; my father depended on her for that.

My mother loved the Lord, and prayed for my brother and me. She also loved my dad very much.

In later years she also wrote a bit of poetry. Here is one example.

FEBRUARY 23, 1963   The below poem was written by mother.

I Cannot Doubt Him [6]
Doubt Him I cannot, can you?
He who has proven so true.
I cannot doubt Him, can you?

Doubt His love so strong,
He who suffered long
There on Calvary, doubt Him,
How can we doubt Him?

Doubt Him and His promises too,
A place by His side eternity through.
All this for me and for you.
I cannot, can you Doubt Him?

What does He ask of you and me?
Faith and trust, even this He supplies.
Forever with us His love abides.
Doubt Him, how can we?
Consider the cost if you will,

That lifeless form on Calvary's hill;
The cost, death, shame and disgrace
As He hung there in our place.

Doubt Him, oh no, I cannot, can you?
Because of this, His home I'll share
Throughout eternity I'll be there.
Doubt Him, oh no! I cannot,
Can you Doubt Him?

When my father was in the Army, my mother would allow my brother and me to play "shoe store" with her shoes. We would bring her high heels downstairs, and as she sat knitting, my brother and I would try the shoes on her feet, and try to sell them to her. She would also allow me to give her a pedicure with a lovely set of foot products. One, in particular that I remember was a very soft "buffer" to make her toenails shine. It was pink. It was so much fun. She would laugh because we tickled her feet as we were trying the shoes on them.

My mother and I would do the dishes together after dinner in the evening, and we would talk. She would wash, and I would dry, and put away. On occasion she would allow me to wash them. That was special. I would talk about school, but mostly about boys. She very highly stressed to me that it was important for me to set "guidelines" in a dating relationship. I did. To this day I need never be ashamed or embarrassed to meet a former boyfriend, for I followed her advice.

Only once do I remember my mother getting very angry with me. We were doing the dishes and I must have said something to her in a rude tone, for she slapped me hard across the mouth. My glasses flew off and broke. I cried. I don't remember any more than that. That was the first and last time something like that took place.

My mother taught herself to play the organ when she was in her 50s. That was quite an accomplishment.

My mother at times got the "blues", as she called it. She would feel a little sad. The only reason I can even imagine for that is that my father had trouble communicating his feelings, and perhaps at times she felt lonely. I always felt the need to make her feel better.

I remember calling her "mommy", "mother", and finally "mom", with the greatest of respect and affection.

She passed away at age 59, my mother, my example in life.

I love you mom, and cherish the times we had together. I wish you could have seen your grandchildren as adults; you would be so proud of them, and you would love the people they married. You also would have adored your great-grandchildren; two girls, and a boy. They would have loved you too.

You are now with Jesus, my father, and many of the people in life whom you influenced by your kindness. You are surrounded by love. Mom, I think perhaps dad was not always able to share himself as deeply as you desired, and you may have felt lonely, but now you are with Jesus, and Jesus is the great communicator. You will never be lonely again. I am happy for you.

I was the last person to see each of my parents alive. My mother died three hours after I left her bedside in January of 1979, and I was with my father when he took his last breath in September of 2009. Though both of my parents were followers of Jesus, and are with Him, both of these times were very sorrowful for me. Those last moments with them are fixed in my mind and heart forever, and I find those last visits painful to recall because it is the last time I saw them here on this earth.

I wish they were still alive so I could say to them, "I love you." I will see them again, however, and the parting will be over.

My Brother

I have a brother. He looks very much like our father. He is a very handsome man. In his mid-70s he still turns the heads of many women. He has acquired some traits from each one of our parents. He is compassionate. He is introverted, doesn't like crowds. He likes order, and is not always tolerant of messiness. He is left-handed. He is very intelligent, and has accomplished a lot in life. He graduated from high school at 17 and entered the Marine Corp. He trained as a paratrooper, and was the one who prepared all the parachutes for the jumpers to use. He is a reader. He is witty. He was a businessman. He was a missionary to Africa. He was a pastor. He has the sweetest of wives, five children, and too many grandchildren and great grandchildren for me to spend time counting. We are similar in appearance. His hair is white, and mine is too. That's about it! His eyes are brown, mine are blue. He is tall and slender, I am, well how should I put it, neither!

When we were young we fought. He is two and a half years younger than I am, and he picked on me. Even tapping on my shoulder would send me screaming, "Mother!"

Sometimes he resented me because I never got in trouble, and I had an easier time in school. I do remember when we were both teenagers sometimes we would sit on his bed and talk things over.

We also had fun together. When we were kids we wrestled, we played softball, and all the other games kids played at that time. I thought it was especially fun to play "cowboys" (with cap gun), and "Indians" (with bow and arrow). I guess now days one is still allowed to say "cowboy", but it is not politically correct to say "Indian". I mean no disrespect.

My brother and I are closer now than when we were younger. Sometimes growing up does that. It is interesting how children growing up in the same family will often view, and remember things differently. That is because we, indeed, are different people.

I love you brother, and I am thankful we are both still here on earth to encourage one another.

During these growing up years I also had the privilege of knowing four of my grandparents, and four of my great-grandparents. I'd like you to meet them.

Grandpa Zarfoss

Grandpa Zarfoss, my favorite, loved music, and I used to listen to his Victrola as Etzio Pinza, a great opera star, would sing. I also remember most of the words to "That Old Black Magic", and "Temptation". Neither of these songs were particularly good for a little girl to hear, for they talk of romance, and troubles of the heart, but it was an age of innocence in the 40s, and I didn't even know what some of the words meant. I do find it curious that both those songs have a melancholy tune, and to this day that is the kind of music that reaches deep into my heart, and pulls a sadness, and longing from it.

Grandpa Zarfoss was an architect, and often when visiting I would find him at his drawing board. He always seemed pleased to see me, and he would allow me to sit at his roll top desk, and look through all the little cubbies. I loved seeing him at his large drawing board working on the design of one of the various churches in York that he designed.

Grandpa Zarfoss also loved roses, and had many varieties which he tended and pruned. He was very proud of his rose beds, and many times when I would visit after he retired, that is where I would find him. Grandpa Zarfoss also like to watch the evening news; John Cameron Swayze, a news broadcaster of the time, was his favorite as was a church program where Bishop Fulton Sheen spoke. I was quiet when visiting if he was watching either of these programs.

My grandfather also liked President Roosevelt, and President Truman; so in my mind, that meant they were good.
Grandpa Zarfoss also make delicious homemade vanilla ice cream, and homemade bread. It was outstanding! Grandpa Zarfoss spent his remaining years in a nursing home, and lived to see his oldest child, my mother die. I only wish when visiting him I would have stopped to recall the part in my life he played, and would have told him how much he meant to me.

I miss him, Grandpa Zarfoss I loved him.

Grandma Zarfoss

Grandma Zarfoss was quiet. She was a good cook. When she was a young girl she wanted to be an artist but there was no money for lessons. When she was in her fifties she finally went to art school, and eventually had a small studio in her basement where she painted in oils. She taught some of the neighborhood ladies how to do the same. Sometimes when I visited that is where she and the others would be. She would set me up and give me the opportunity to work on a still life.

Because of her influence I've been able to do a few paintings, one of which hangs in my son's kitchen, though that particular skill fell more to my daughter, Melody.

Grandma had a compassionate heart, and I can remember her feeding the "bums", as we called them back in the forties. When they were hungry they knew where to stop. She would fill their plates with hot food, and they would sit on the back porch, eat, and feel satisfied when they left.

When she dressed for church or a social event she was very classy looking; at other times she looked just like a typical housewife of the 1940s and 1950s dressed in skirt and blouse, not always matching, by the standard of the day. When it came to Sundays, it was hat, gloves, and heels for church. My grandparents would not believe how casual the dress is today for church going.

Grandma Zarfoss was also a seamstress and worked in York, at Rogers, which sold fine dresses. She was their alterations lady, as well as saleslady.

Grandma Zarfoss also loved to eat the leftover jelly, or whatever was left in the dishes, after dinner. She continued to do this even after getting diabetes later in life. Hmm, I have no doubt where my love of food comes from. I loved her "Schnitz and Knepp"! Oh, that Pennsylvania cooking! Memories, sweet memories.

I miss you, Grandma Zarfoss I wish you were still here. You would be pleased to know that the many paintings you worked so tirelessly at now hang in the homes of your family. You were a beautiful artist, and you were given that gift by the first and greatest Artist ever.

Grandma Coldren

Grandma Coldren wanted to be a singer as a young girl. Her father would not allow that. This was in the early 1900s and I guess that wasn't proper then. Grandma Coldren could play the piano, but for reasons I never knew, Grandfather Coldren did not want her playing when he was home. When I would visit, and he was gone we would play for each other.

I find it sad that both things she enjoyed she was denied the privilege of sharing with others.

Grandma Coldren was beautiful, and she collected teacups.

I always thought she preferred my brother over me, and I know she felt more comfortable with him because she herself had three boys. When she was very near death she said a curious thing to me out of the blue. She said, "I know you think I never loved you, but I did." I do know I could sense that she preferred my brother, but it may have just been that she knew better how to relate to him.

When I would visit Grandma Coldren overnight she would make tea and toast with blackberry jam for me in the morning. We would sit together and enjoy it. Blackberry jam is still my favorite jam. She also loved raspberry ice cream.

Grandma Coldren would, after doing the evening dishes, drink a small glass of water which always sat by the sink, and then when I was visiting, we would go out back, sit in a lawn chair, and visit with her neighbor, Miss King. It was kind of a ritual; one I think on with pleasant thoughts.

I miss you Grandma Coldren I wish you would have had the opportunity to become a singer.

Grandpa Coldren

Grandpa Coldren was not someone I enjoyed being around. He thought teasing was fun, but it was usually at the expense of others who were vulnerable. He was also very prejudiced and used some nasty words about people. One thing I learned from him was that I never wanted to speak so unkindly about people because they were different. So, I guess in that way he taught me something valuable.

Grandpa did, however, make the best oysters I ever ate. But when he died, his recipe died with him. He never shared it with my grandmother, nor anyone else that I am aware of. He was a cook in the army in World War 1.

Grandpa also taught me to play Solitaire, the only time I really enjoyed being with him.

I also remember four of my great-grandparents, and loved them. Two of them were city folks and two were country folks, right down to the old outhouse! I feel very blessed to have known each one.

And of course, like many of you, I had a myriad of aunts, uncles, and cousins.

I would say I came from honorable, and God-fearing people. The curious thing is that I never heard my grandparents talk about the Lord, or their faith. I wonder why.

3
The Sowing of a Seed

1958   My mother gives me a book of poetry by Annie Johnson Flint, the only poet whose book I've ever read. I don't have a clue why she bought it for me. I don't remember us ever discussing poetry. Though I wrote that one poem when I was 15, I had not developed the desire any further than that, at least not that I recall. I am not a fan of poetry. The one exception being is if I know you, and you write a poem, I am pleased and honored if you share it with me. Poetry can reveal how a person thinks, and what is in their heart. Speaking face to face can do that as well, but for some people deep feelings are more easily expressed in the written word. I know words come easier to me when I am writing them, then when I speak them out loud. I don't know why this is; I only know I feel less self-conscious.

My mother did not realize she had been used of the Lord to sow a seed that would be a great treasure to me. It is my hope that you will not only travel this path of life-poetry with me, but that you will find that God Almighty walked with me, and He desires to walk with, and encourage you.

"'He who sows the good seed is the Son of Man'
(New King James Version, Matt. 13.37)."

1959   I am 17 and in my senior year of high school.

I am an average student at this time; my academic abilities being somewhat hindered by insecurity. Through-out grade school I excelled, but when I got to Jr. high my grades plummeted drastically. I've never been sure why. Perhaps it was the experience of seeing a man expose himself to me that happened when I was 12. Maybe at that age I just couldn't process how to handle it, and though I told my mother, her telling me that he was sick, just wasn't enough. I probably needed to talk about it more, but would have been too embarrassed to bring the event up again. I really don't know for sure, but in grade school I got mostly A's with an occasional B. Now I was getting B's C's, and an occasional failing mark. I even failed a marking period in Home Economics, and also in music. How can I explain that? I really can't, at least not with any definitive explanation.

I was well liked in school, but not really what I would call popular. There were things the in-gang did that I wasn't part of so there was a bit of a wall between us. I was trusted though and on occasion some of the girls would talk with me about something that bothered them, usually about their boyfriends. The funny thing is I had very little experience with boys, so I really wasn't an expert. I think they just wanted someone to talk with.

Though I did not excel necessarily at anything, I did love being in the Junior play, and the Senior operetta. I loved music, and played the glockenspiel in the high school band. It was comical to see me marching in the field because at 5'1" you really couldn't find me behind that tall instrument. In one of the photographs of the band you see what looks like a headless person playing the instrument. But I was pretty good because I played the piano, and finding the right keys to hit was easy. I also enjoyed anything that involved writing, right down to the basic art of forming the letters; I still love to have a writing implement in my hand, preferring pen over pencil. That is not always the wisest choice, but now a days we have correction fluid - Yea! I also enjoyed gym class where I could definitely hold my own.

When I was in high school I was part of a Bible club and I carried my Bible. Because I did not like being different and calling attention to myself, this was uncomfortable for me. It accentuated my difference. I stood out.

Christians are called to be different, aren't we?

February 5, 1959

Closer
Closer draw me Lord, to Thee –
Closer yet I pray
Until I know Thee as I want
Draw closer every day.

Until I know Your grief and pain,
Your sorrow and Your care,

Your heart that longs for dying souls –
Oh, let me have a share.

Until I know Your sufferings long,
Until I know Your love so strong –
I know now that I belong
Still closer, closer, Lord to Thee.

"'That I may know Him, and the power of His
resurrection, and the fellowship of His sufferings,
being made conformable unto His death' (King
James Version, Phil. 3.10)."

This verse is admirable, and desirable, until one finds himself
needing to practice it. Then, as you will hear me mention later on, this
is when the "rubber meets the road".

"'Now this is the confidence we have in Him, that if
we ask anything according to His will, He hears us.
And we know that if He hears us, whatever we ask,
we know we have the petitions that we have asked
of Him' (New King James Version, 1 John 5.14-15)."

In the aforementioned poem I asked the Lord to draw me
closer and allow me to experience some of His pain. I did not realize
the means He would use to answer that request. In my experience, it
was living in a difficult marriage which caused me a lot of emotional
anxiety and pain. The Lord used my desire to share His pain, but being
human I just did not realize what avenue that request would take me
on. When we request something of the Lord, it always involves a
measure of trust.

4
Summertime, and the Livin' Ain't Easy

AUGUST 1959   I am 18. Graduation over; now what?

As I grew to be a teenager the only thing I wanted to do was get married and have a family. This was my dream. The man I married and I would have a loving relationship, shared goals, and close communication with one another. There would be lots of togetherness, romance, and yes, sex. It was such a perfect dream, and seemed so possible. There really weren't a whole lot of other things that appealed to me. I did not yet realize how very much I loved to write, and I had no desire to be a secretary, nurse, or teacher. These were the occupations young women had to choose from in the 1950s. I was not prepared for anything else, and then all of a sudden, the "anything else", in other words, graduation, was here! My mother wanted me to go to Moody Bible Institute in Chicago, but the thought of being so far from home scared me, and I had a boyfriend, and he did not want me to go to college. I, however, chose to attend Lancaster School of the Bible. I fit right in, and I loved every minute of the four years I spent there. I would do the same thing all over again, though on second thought it probably would have been wiser for me to go further from home.

There was a young man who entered Bible school the same time I did. The first time I saw him was during the introduction of freshman. He was head and shoulders above all the boys I knew at that time. I really liked him. He had so many of the qualities I found attractive. He was musical, smart, a leader, articulate, well spoken, and handsome. He never knew how much I liked him because I was afraid to let him know. I didn't think I was good enough for him, whatever that means. I've always regretted playing that "hiding my feelings" game. I haven't seen or spoken with him since 1963. I still wonder what his life path was like. I would wish for the opportunity to just sit and talk.

Did you ever play that kind of game? Do you regret it?

Live Your Life In Me
Walk with me, Jesus, day by day.
Walk with me, Jesus, along the way.
Talk to me, Jesus, sweet and low.
Show me, dear Jesus, which way to go.

Love through me, Jesus, each one I meet.
Love through me, Jesus, 'til You they seek.
Draw me close, Jesus, until You alone I see.
Draw close to me, Jesus, live Your life in me.

5
All I Have To Do Is Dre-e-e-e-am

1960   I am 19 and dating the man I would one day marry.
I began dating another freshman this year. He was also a
student at the Bible School I was attending. I had dated him for a
month in high school, and then returned to my former boyfriend, but
that relationship came to an end, and so in the early fall of 1960 my
high school friend and I reconnected. There was so much about him
that I liked. He was fun, and funny. We had really good conversations;
he was very accepting; and above all, I felt safe. And he thought I was
wonderful! It sounds like a match made in heaven, but as we grew
closer I sensed that something didn't feel quite right. This I believe was
caution number one. I believe the Holy Spirit was speaking to me
through my unsettled feeling. Perhaps my dream as a young girl to be
married and have a family made it hard for me to hear Him. Perhaps
hearing Him took second place in my heart.

As I look at this picture above, I realize how out of balance it
is. I avoided and pretended not to care for one young man because I
feared not being able to measure up, and I married someone who
thought I was wonderful. Somewhere in there something is out of
whack. You can try to figure it out if you wish.

A thankful heart can be a great blessing. Recognizing how
much the Lord has given us by giving Himself, and daily supplying us
with good, is the basis for the following poem.

JUNE 1961

Thank-You
Dear Father in Heaven,
I thank you for blessings large and small,
But, most of all, for the love of Your precious Son;
Who died for each, for all.

May I walk each day with Him –
Always be kind, and true;
And may I always remember
To bring my thanks to You.

"'Thanks be unto God for His unspeakable gift' (King James Version, 2 Cor. 9.15)!"

Jesus Christ is This Unspeakable Gift.

I was 20 years old when I wrote "Molded Vessel". I sadly smile when I read my request of the Lord to help me not to stumble. I stumble so many times along the road of life. This is because I am human, and continue to have many lessons to learn; two of them being; life does not always provide a smooth path; and every life has value, and purpose.

The amazing thing is; Almighty God walks my walk with me. He never stumbles; He is never lost. He always does what it right. We continue to walk together.

OCTOBER 11, 1961

Molded Vessel
Make me, Lord, to be more like Thee –
A useable vessel, Thy servant to be.
Melt me and mold me as the potter does the clay;
Use this vessel in Your way today.

Keep me from stumbling along this road;
Help me to bear my present-day load.
And if I fall and fail as I do,
Teach me, dear Lord – this I ask of You.

It is here I want to insert a poem from 1980.

1980

The Potter and the Clay
For He is God - He made me.

He is the Potter - I am the clay.
Yes, He is God - He made me
To be a vessel to use today.

"'Then I went down to the potter's house, and behold he wrought a work on the wheels. And the vessel that he made of clay was marred in the hand of the potter: so he made it again another vessel, as seemed good to the potter to make' (King James Version, Jer. 18.3-4)."

"'Saith the Lord, Behold as the clay is in the potter's hand, so are ye in mine' (King James Version, Jer. 18.6)."

The Almighty God made me and knows all about me. The same is true of you. He is the Creator, the Master Artist; it is He, alone, who knows what we need to be, so He can use us. I know this is true. I believe it. But allowing Him to take charge is not always agreeable to me, because sometimes it goes against my own desires, and sometimes it hurts. I have found through experience that it is better to do things his way. His hard is less hard than me choosing my own way.

OCTOBER, 1961

Burden in Hand
Give me a burden for one soul today;
Give me the words to speak in Your way.
Give me Your wisdom, and show me Your plan;
Help me to lead this soul by the hand.

The only thing I remember about writing the following poem is that my boyfriend and I were having a problem of some sort, and I knew we needed help.

DECEMBER 1961

The Drive
Lord, there's a long drive ahead of us, -

A drive we alone can't make.
We need Your hand to guide us –
To show us the road to take.

May we follow Your light night and day,
No matter what the dangers are.
Please keep us on the way, Lord,
Whether we are near or far.

You are our Driver, Lord,
And we Your followers be.
Help us to be faithful
In our life long drive with Thee.

The Lord knew there would be a very long drive ahead. He always knows what is going on. He always knows, and goes before us, and goes with us, sometimes with tears in His eyes.

One of my favorite Bible verses is in Exodus. My husband and I memorized verses of scripture together when we were dating. It is strange that this particular verse is the only one I remember us learning, though I know there were many others. It was the first one we memorized.

"'Behold, I send an Angel before thee, to keep thee in the way, and to bring thee into the place which I have prepared' (King James Version, Exod. 23.20)."

6
Dreams in the Desert

1962   I am 21. It is Christmastime.

Christmas is such a beautiful time of the year. It is especially beautiful when you have someone special to spend it with. This was the month my boyfriend asked me to marry him. We went to a restaurant in Camp Hill, Pa, called The Dutch Pantry. There was a small candle on each table, and we sat by a window. My 'almost' fiancé bought me a little Dutch doll, dressed in red, as a keepsake. After dinner, we went to Penn Grove Camp Ground where he got down on one knee and asked me to marry him. I said "yes", and he gave me a lovely diamond which I proudly showed off to my mother, and her best friend Elli, that evening. My father saw it later when he came home from work.

I failed to mention that though my parents liked my fiancé, they did not want us to marry. When my fiancé asked my dad if he could marry me, my dad's response was, "Well, I guess I don't have a choice!" I remember my then fiancé telling me this like it was yesterday. This was caution number two, and this one I wasn't interested in hearing. It is unfortunate that I did not have the kind of relationship with my father, as I had with my mother, and that made talking with him about personal things uncomfortable. We were not close. We never really sat down and had any heart-to-heart conversation about anything at all, so at this very important time in my life, I could not really hear his concern; I only thought of it as control. I was anxious to get out and begin my "dream life". The parents of my fiancé, I think on the other hand were delighted because he was marrying a Christian girl. They were aware of some problems he had, and I suspect they thought I might be the answer to them. At the time I did not realize this. I loved his family. There were six siblings. What fun! I felt so at ease and accepted around them. As I am writing this book my former husband's siblings are all still living, the eldest turned 78 this year. I still love them, and still consider them family.

Allow me to back track for a moment. Do you remember me mentioning my mother's best friend, Elli? Well Elli waited until the age of 39 before the Lord brought a husband to her. Today there are many young women who wait until their 30s to get married, but back in the 1940s most women married in their 20s, so waiting some 15 extra years was not easy for her. Waiting can have its benefits. Being in a hurry seldom does.

DECEMBER 27, 1962

Tender Face of Love
Lord, draw me close now,
And leave me look into Your face.
Let me catch a glimpse
Of Your tender, loving grace.

Help me to know You love me;
Help me Your love to others show.

Our wedding was set for August 1963. We would both graduate from Lancaster School of the Bible in June, and then after we were married we would be leaving for Grace Collage in Indiana where my husband was going to get a degree. The Bible school we graduated from offered only a diploma in those days. It is now a fully accredited college.

A few days before we were married I was sitting on a gold French Provincial chair by the fireplace in my parents living room. My Bible was open on my lap, and I was searching. I had no peace about the marriage and I was asking the Lord to show me what to do about it. He had already done so twice; I didn't see that then. I was blinded by my dream of a perfect marriage. This was the third time I was cautioned, and still I did not recognize His voice, or His leading. He was not surprised, but I can only imagine He was sad.

If you are experiencing this kind of doubt about anything in life, it does not automatically mean you should not proceed, but probably means you should wait until things become clear. Hard to do, but worth it in the long run.

By now I knew my parents had already put a lot of money into the wedding; the gown, the flowers, the invitations, etc. and I felt I couldn't call it off; I think I was too embarrassed to do so, though I momentarily considered it. I really didn't know if I wanted to. I was so confused.

Confused. And confusion is never of the Lord. His desire is never to confuse, or trick us. Sometimes in life we just don't wait long enough for His answer.

"'Show me your ways, O Lord; teach me Your paths'
(New King James Version, Ps. 25.4)."

A verse given me many years later by my daughter.

"Teach me Your way, O Lord, and lead me in a
smooth path, because of my enemies' (New King
James Version, Ps. 27.11)."

Yes, even one's natural desires can be an enemy.

My parents had no idea I was struggling with this decision. It was foolish on my part to keep it from them. Perhaps it was pride, fear of their reaction, or simply not knowing what to do, I'm not sure. I don't think I even considered talking it over with them. We never really sat down and talked about much of anything. They loved me, and cared about me, but talking things over together just wasn't what we did. When I was a child I was told what to do, and what not to do, and somewhere in the years of growing up, when that was no longer necessary, communication was limited to do what we were each doing. There was a gap in communication, and none of us realized it. It happens in many families. If this is a possibility in your family, perhaps you could look at it and endeavor to do differently.

During the months of our engagement my fiancé and I took turns wondering if we were making the right decision. When one was unsure, the other was sure, and so we seesawed back and forth. This was caution number four. The plans continued to unfold up to this moment by the fireplace. I was frustrated because I thought I was not getting an answer, so I closed my Bible and decided to go through with the wedding. I can easily put myself back there in that chair and hear the sound of my Bible closing. My fiancé no longer expressed any concern, and I just did not realize until many years later that all the time, and in a variety of ways, the Holy Spirit was trying to give me the answer through my lack of peace.

The enemy of God used my God given desire for a husband and a family to blind me. He played havoc with our lives in an attempt to accomplish what he wanted. He wanted to destroy my life, my future, my husband's life, and our children's lives. He wanted to bring dishonor on God's church, and on His name. He was able to do that, but only for a season. Because God is bigger. Always remember that; God is bigger.

7

Here Comes the Bride,
Here Comes the Groom

AUGUST 16, 1963   I am 22. I become a wife.

Following graduation from Bible school, we were married two months later.

It was a beautiful ceremony, and after hours of opening gifts at the reception, we left for our week-long honeymoon to Rehoboth Beach. The next week we went back to my parents and loaded up a U-Haul with our many wedding gifts. and after saying good bye to both our families, we headed for Indiana, where my husband would be attending college, as well as looking for work. We didn't know where we would be living, but it was an adventure we both were willing to undertake. It was a very exciting time. A new life. Our life. Doubts temporarily dissipated with this new adventure ahead of us.

I still have a record of some of the expenses my parents paid for my wedding gown on a typed up written paper. I think you might enjoy seeing the itemized list.

The purchases were made at the Pat Morgart Bridal Shop in Dover, Pennsylvania. The shop is no longer there, and Pat Morgart is no longer living.

Here is the letter she wrote to me on April 12, 1963

Dear Barbara,

I would like to thank you for your check in the amount of $30.00, which I received as a deposit on your wedding gown, veil and headpiece. I hope you will be very well satisfied with your outfit, and I am enclosing your receipt.

So you will know just what the prices of each item are, I am listing them as follows:

#499 Lace Portrait wedding gown $89.00
#743 Fine Pearl Crown and Veil $19.50

Subtotal $108.50
Penna. Sales Tax $4.34
Total $112.34
Less deposit 4/12/63 $30.00

Balance $82.84

*Thank you again, and you will be hearing from me
just as soon as the gown arrives.*

Sincerely (Ms. Mogart's signature)

I am sure now, one would pay at least $1,000.00 for the gown and accessories I had. Two "something specials" came out of the expenses of my wedding gown. In 1984, my daughter wore it, and in 2013, my youngest granddaughter wore it. The money my parents paid for the gown was used two times over, making it well worth the purchase. I would have loved for my mother to see the girls in my wedding gown, but she had already died.

Our first apartment was in the basement of a large apartment building. It had one big room which was divided in half by our couch, and trunk. One side was the kitchen, and the other side, the living room. The bedroom was surrounded by cinder blocks painted a pale green, and the bathroom meant a trip to the garage! The rent was $60.00 a month. Both of us loved fixing things up and so we set to work making this our home. We never had a problem agreeing on how to do this. We enjoyed the process of decorating together. We had our new wedding gifts crammed into every nook and cranny we could find! While my husband looked for a job, I spent the days writing thank you cards to friends and family for the beautiful wedding gifts they had given us. Once my parents came to visit us for the weekend and slept on the pull out couch we had in our living room. His parents also came at another time.

My husband found a full-time job at a foundry, and worked 4:00 p.m. to 12:00 a.m. He went to school during the day. I got a job as a nurse's aide within walking distance from the apartment. We had one car, so when I had need of it to go for groceries I would take him to work, and then go pick him up at midnight. He worked by himself during those late hours, and would usually show me the various metal things he was working on. Then we would drive home together.

I remember our first big argument was when we could not agree on the purchase of life insurance. I wanted it, he didn't. After my father left the railroad he sold insurance, and of course he had insurance on his family, and therefore believed it to be important. I never heard of such a thing as not having insurance, and it was inconceivable to me that he didn't want to buy into a plan. Had I been mature enough I would have just bided some time while praying about his decision, instead of being so sure that I was right. Being right is not always the most important consideration. Possibly, being right can be interpreted as desiring control.

8
Silencing the Scream

1963   I am 22 and feeling trapped.

A few weeks into our marriage, as I lay alone on the bed, I sobbed, and said, "Oh Lord, what have I done!!! What have I done"! I was brokenhearted. I was confused, and I felt rejected. Something in our relationship was very wrong. I believe it was at this time I began to pretend to others that our relationship was good, and I began to feel trapped. As far as I was concerned I was married for life, and pretending was the only thing at this point that I knew to do. I think I also may have pretended to myself that things would work out, but secretly, marriage began to take on a new meaning for me: trapped. That was September of 1963. I felt trapped for life. I don't know how he felt.

It wasn't that my husband and I didn't talk about our problems, we did, sometimes for hours, and then I would feel better, hopeful, but there was a major secret under the surface, and so we both were experiencing false hope, and the peace was never for long. Things were now moving in a slow downward spiral.

To all those whose path we crossed daily, everything looked okay. I think we almost fooled ourselves.

Isn't that the way Satan works? He doesn't want secrets to be brought into the light. He uses the darkness to his own advantage. And he did. He is most certainly the enemy of our souls. He seeks to blind us, and sad to say, he often does.

But it does not have to be a permanent state of darkness.

Are you caught in this same place? Holler for help! Please; holler until someone hears you! Don't let your pride get in the way.

God always desires for us to be brought into the light; to walk in the Light. And as we are seeking Him, He will break through the darkest hours our soul may enter, and shed His light and truth on our heart.

Sometimes it takes a long time for Him to get through to us. Sometimes He keeps extending His grace, as He waits.

> "'In thy light shall we see light' (King James Version, Ps. 36.9b)."

> "'God is light, and in him is no darkness at all' (King James Version, 1 John 1.5b)."

9
Living in the Storm

I remember as a teen telling a friend there was absolutely no reason for a man and woman to get a divorce as long as they were able to talk things out. I was so sure that was all it took. Just talk things out. I assumed the talking, the reasoning, would produce a logical, helpful answer, and the problem would be solved. Talking things out proved not to be the answer for us. Talking was not enough.

When I was a teenager I also reasoned that when I got married I wouldn't have someone telling me what to do, or how I needed to act, and then I would finally be able to relax, and be free of stomach pains. My stomach often felt in knots when I was growing up. At one point as a teen I went to the doctors because I was sure I had stomach cancer. The doctor said it was stress, not cancer. That put my mind at ease, but didn't really help the problem. I was looking for the freedom to think for myself, and just be allowed to be. I didn't realize that when one is married sometimes it means "obedience" to a higher authority. I thought it meant freedom! It wasn't that I had a desire to do things that were wrong, I just wanted a chance to be out from under control.

Here is a poem written in 1986, age 45, as I reflected on my feelings from childhood to adulthood. I mean no disrespect to either of my parents, for I loved them then and even more now, and appreciate the many lessons they taught me. I believe their intent was always for my good.

It was just that I felt I needed room to breathe and grow, and they, I'm sure, didn't want me to make any mistakes. We never talked much about feelings.

APRIL 21, 1986

As Positioned
I feel like I shall never be

Able to identify me
One-by-one I'm stripped away
And find I fade with yesterday.

Sometimes I feel as I was
An infant long ago
Clean and sweet and turned out right,
As positioned, I did grow.

I did not cry, did not pout,
Did what I was told to
And all they wanted in me came out,
As positioned, so I grew.

When my brother came along
And made my mother cry
And made my daddy angry,
I kept busy, being I.

He would get in trouble
And say things out of the way
I would just keep being there
The same as yesterday.

They could always count on me
To say and be real good
Exactly what they wanted
Just the way I should.

Please your mommy, don't make her cry
She can count on you.
Please your daddy, don't make him mad,
Be just right, please do, please do.

Then one day I heard in church
A message on sin and hell.
Up to the alter my parents went
And wished I had gone as well.
I don't remember why I fought,

Except I had been good
And now my good not good enough
Required another "should."

Over and over each night of each week
He pressured and pulled the souls He did seek,
Fear raged within me and took its control
And down to the alter went me with my soul.

Everyone my parents knew
Looked at me through shaded eyes
And I increased the saccharin product
Of their pleased and wanting lies.

Filled with good intentions
I grew as I was grown,
My heart in absent intervention
Knew as I grew, I grew alone.

Please your mommy, don't make her cry,
She can count on you.
Please your daddy, don't make him mad,
Add to this the Lord, please do.

Read your Bible, pray each day,
Live your life anew,
If you don't you'll surely pay,
For He is watching you.

Witness everywhere you go
Down with movies and the dance.
No more cards where monies flow,
And don't give boys too much a chance.

Do not fail, do not flirt,
Be at every meeting.
Think right thoughts or you'll be hurt,
And never stoop to cheating.

Do not smoke and do not drink,
Use your head, stop and think!
Don't be mean, and don't be rude,
And never, ever say things crude!

The Lord is watching how you grow
And then this promise still,
Worse than all you'll ever know
Is living your life outside His will!

And so in all my days of youth
I kept the rules required of me
And gave to others half the truth
And half the truth I'd yet to see.

And dumb enough I was to think
That the rules I had obeyed
Would provide me with the cup to drink
Of happiness today.

Add to this confusion, anger, and desire,
Each a forbidden expression and so we fan the fire.
Within my heart I carried plans of all that I would be
And dreamed the man I married would love and
understand me.

Here comes the bride, here comes the groom,
Here comes their life of private doom.
I give to you, and you give to me
Baskets full of "yet to be."

The time a mere nothing,
The distance great as space
The two who were lonely
Shared baskets of waste.

I can't figure out what happened,
Why things turned out this way
We were once the children

Conceived in yesterday.

Please your mommy, though she's dead, please your
daddy, do;
Please the Lord, and the man you wed, but be in fear
of pleasing you.
Every decision carries its weight as in the days of my
youth,
Frozen in time now growing late, I still await the
moment of truth.

It seems to me that one of the reasons my husband married me was because I had a good reputation, and because he thought that I was someone who could help him with his problem. I wonder, if to him, marriage seemed like his final chance to free himself. His very basic belief about himself was that he was no good. He never was able to believe anything other than that. He never let go of that lie of Satan. There was no way I could convince him otherwise. He spent much of his life trying to prove his point.

Many years later I heard about living under the umbrella. I was out of the umbrella of my husband's protection; there just wasn't one, and he was out of God's. We were entering, and began living in the storms.

There were, of course, other reasons we married. I think a big one was Hope! We each hoped marriage would make up for the lack that we both felt in our hearts. We both wanted to belong.

10
The Graduation That Wasn't

1965   I am 24.

In 1965, about two weeks before graduation, there was an incident at college, and my husband was told to leave. He would not be graduating. This happened one week before our baby was to be born. I was devastated, and scared beyond words. I told my parents, and my mother said they were not surprised at what happened. They knew something I did not know, or suspected something, or heard something. My father wanted the marriage annulled. I would not even consider that. In all the years they were alive, I never asked them what they knew. I don't know why. We were given a month to leave our apartment, for the news had reached our landlord. I knew I could not fall apart because I was about to have a baby to care for. I saw no choice except to be strong. I believed we could lick this! I still had hope. He, I think, just lived on automatic. I think he, too, was scared. I also wonder if he expected nothing else from or for himself but defeat. It was easier than accepting the truth that God made him for more than this.

11
A Song is Born in the Desert

MAY 5, 1965   I am 24. Our daughter is born.
She was the most beautiful baby I had ever seen. She was "sunshine and song" in the words of a poet, and I was absolutely thrilled with her! When her daddy came into the hospital room after seeing her, his first words were, "She's beautiful!" We brought her home in three days, and below is a poem I wrote while I watched her sleep in her bassinet.

Melody
Dear, sweet little golden girl, baby born of love –
Sleeping in your wonderland, Heaven up above.

Mommy watching over your precious little form
Lying here so peacefully in jammies soft and warm.

Daddy smiles with eyes of love at his little golden girl
treasuring all the joy you bring –
You are our richest pearl.

"The kingdom of heaven is like unto a merchant
man, seeking goodly pearls: who, when he had
found one pearl of great price, went and sold all that
he had and bought it' (King James Version, Matt.
13.45)." (My daughter is a "pearl of great price").

I am extremely proud of my daughter. She was a beautiful baby at birth, and she still is beautiful. She has a compassionate heart, and a love for people. She, along with her husband have frequently opened their home to people in need. She is a good listener, and an intelligent woman. She has written some beautiful poetry, and loves music. This year she wrote a praise song for the people in her church.

She has said I was the one who taught her to sing alto. I don't remember consciously doing that, but am proud she attributes that to me. She has the ability to paint and draw. She is the mother of two daughters and now the grandmother of four little ones. She loves the Lord and desires to do His will. She has been through a lot physically and emotionally, and has more than survived! She is a princess warrior!

I mentioned that my daughter likes to write. Below is a poem she wrote about her little grandsons. One is six, and the other two. She also has a baby granddaughter, and in the new year will have a yet to be known, fourth grandchild.

JUNE 8, 2017

The Noise of Boys [3]
The noise of boys and all their toys:
They're joyous joys, but oh, the noise!
They romp and stomp, and clomp and shout;
Bring germs and worms inside the house!
When day is done I'm all worn out!

Then washed and fed and tucked in bed,
With stories, prayers, a kiss on the head,
Their smiles sweet are such a treat!
And oh, so peaceful as they sleep!
And drift to dreams as night grows deep.

Then sun, fun, run, a new day starts;
The joys, the noise, these boys!
These little boys are in my heart!

Isn't that precious? How wonderful to have a grandmother who loves the noise of boys!

FEBRUARY 12, 1991   I found in my Amplified Bible the following verse which was underlined for daughter and son-in-law. I believe they have exemplified this unity as they desire to help others.

"'Fill up and complete my joy by living in harmony and being of the same mind and one in purpose, having the same love, being in full accord and of one harmonious mind and intention' (Amplified, Phil. 2.2)."

12
If at First You Don't Succeed Cry, and Cry Again

At the end of May in 1965 when I was well enough, the three of us came back to York and lived with my parents. While living with them my husband was involved in another incident which made its way into the local newspaper. I can only imagine the embarrassment my parents felt. I accompanied my father-in-law to the jail where bail was posted for my husband, and went back to coping; my husband went back to work. He was able to cope by keeping busy. Since his name and address were in the paper his employer was aware of what had happened. I remember how concerned we were that he would lose his job. My husband was excellent at what he did, so his boss kept him on. I remember how very grateful I was that he showed my husband mercy. He was of the Jewish faith, and I wrote him a thank you letter. I felt a bond toward him because of his great kindness. But he could not have been merciful except that the Lord put it in his heart.

My husband was very remorseful, and ashamed because he had been caught. That gave me hope. So onward we went. The harmful thing was that the seed of distrust was growing by leaps and bounds in my heart.

It was at this time that my father said we needed to find a place of our own because dealing with this kind of embarrassment was just too hard on my mother. So, we set out to find an apartment, and move.

It was also during this time my mother told us about a Christian psychologist who had just began his practice in the Harrisburg area. My husband and I made an appointment and spent much money, time, and self-analysis during the next 20 some years trying to save our marriage. That did not work either.

A year later, when our lease was up we bought a mobile home. That was in 1966. I began encouraging my husband to see if he could return to college and finish in good standing. We had a neighbor who was willing to keep an eye on our mobile home for the last semester at college, and once again, in January of 1968, we left for college in Indiana. At this point our little girl was two and a half. We rented a third-floor apartment.

Sometimes I wonder about the trauma our parents experienced.

DECEMBER 1966

Lonely Hearts Everywhere
I see no people in this world, but many lonely hearts-
Hearts in need of touching each other,
in need of knowing someone cares.
What about you my heart, what is your need,
And who can meet it:
And whose need can you meet?

MARCH 1968 We were in the car, and we were not speaking. I don't remember why. I can only see myself staring out the passenger side window and writing this poem in my head.

Together, Apart
Here we sit, the two of us-
Each with his own secret thoughts-
Each not knowing himself, or the other,
Yet desiring to know both.

What is it that keeps us apart?
My heart, is it you, or the other?
No, it is a misunderstanding.

My husband did finish college and got his degree. Our parents both drove to Indiana to attend his graduation. That was an accomplishment for him, and I'm glad he did it.

Oh, the grace God gives to His people! We all need His grace. Is there someone in your life that you could extend this grace towards? Someone who has hurt you, someone who has failed? You? We each need grace. It enables the desire to make the changes we need to make. It gives God the permission to work in our heart.

My husband had applied for a pastor position in a Brethren church in the state of Nebraska before graduation; and following graduation we were invited to go see the church. That was such an enjoyable trip. He preached a sermon while we were there so the people could make a decision. We also were shown the parsonage where we would live if he was invited to permanently come. It was a large country type home. I loved it, and was excited about the possibility of my husband taking on this position. He was a very good Bible teacher. One sweet thing I remember is our three-year-old daughter quietly coloring a picture of a turtle as we sat in the last pew in the church while my husband preached.

From Nebraska, we went back home to Pennsylvania, and our mobile home, and waited. It was after a couple of weeks that the letter came inviting my husband to come as pastor. We never went. Moving to another state doesn't get rid of problems. It can only provide a new stage on which to pretend.

13
Counseling

I want to first say that we had a Godly, Christian Psychologist who was used in both our lives. Unless you have an addiction, or live with someone who does, it is impossible to know the toll it can take on everyone's life. No one escapes unscathed. I thought I would go out of my mind. I wonder sometimes if my husband and I somehow split ourselves in two, emotionally in order to cope. "But, God". There is nothing more to say; "But, God". Some of you understand what I mean when I say, "But, God". From 1968-1984 we saw the counselor on an individual basis. These were weekly visits for quite a long time, and then as time went on, monthly. Sometimes there were months between appointments, and sometimes a few years, but in the 24 years we were married, we were never finished. (Counseling even continued after that for a number of years).

During these years there was much introspection, much searching of heart. I am so grateful for the gift of poetry the Lord gave. I poured out all my questionings, my anger, my sadness, my hopelessness into words. I seldom read the poetry out loud during that time, except to a few people, including my husband. He too, was doing some writing of his own. You will see in my poems the turmoil, the questioning, the searching for acceptance, and the deep outpouring of what was inside. Some of you will understand.

14
Home Ownership

March 1969   I am 27. We bought our first home.
        We paid $7,900.00 It was a small two-bedroom brick home in a nice neighborhood. The previous owners had two police dogs who were kept in one of the bedrooms when the owners went away. Can you visualize what the windowsills, and floors looked like! The whole house was a real mess! Dirty, and with hardwood floors that were completely ruined by those dogs. Grandfather Zarfoss bought us a rug for the living room. We choose a beautiful sunshine yellow. This may not have been the most practical choice because that was our main way of entry, but it sure was a lovely color. We set to work together and made it a charming place to live. We always enjoyed working together. My husband was a painter, and had a good eye for color. He was always willing to fix things up to look nice. I will forever have very fond memories of those times together. I know for sure we changed the color of our rooms more than the average person! Some painters only paint for other people, but he painted for us just as much.
        We papered our little girl's room in large colorful flowers; red and yellow if my memory is correct.
        The kitchen we did in aqua and green flowers, big flowers as well, for the 1970s were approaching and all those large, bright patterns and colors were in vogue.

May 13, 1969

Bedtime Tears
Tonight, I sent my little girl to bed
With tears in her eyes;
I was so tired and paid no attention to her cries.
I am sad.
I want to hold her. There is tomorrow.
Thank you, Lord, for tomorrows.

Even now, I feel so sad when I read this. I don't know why she was upset, and I don't know why I didn't fix what was wrong. Maybe I tried. I think I was wearing out.

MAY 21, 1969

Meet Me
Have you ever been in the place of waiting:
Utter despair;
Frazzled nerves, weary heart, beyond faith,
Beyond care?

You could not seem to go this way or that way;
Sat still, felt defeated, unbelieving;
Meet me; I'm there now.

Have you ever been that tired?
Have you ever been in that place of despair?

I am so thankful the Lord was with me all the time.
Eight weeks after we bought our home, we found out we were expecting another baby. Our little girl was four at this time and so I thought how wonderful it would be to also have a little boy. That was before it was so easy to find out what the sex of your child was.

15
"Peace" Cometh in the Desert

February 12, 1970   I am 28. Our son is born.

I was so happy to now have a little boy. Don't people call this a million-dollar family; meaning both a boy and a girl? I loved the idea of being able to say, "son". I still remember how tender I felt toward him. That is a feeling that never goes away, and one to be cherished forever. His name means "peace". Our peace came while walking in the desert.

He and I had to stay in the hospital for 10 days due to the fact that he had jaundice, and I had lost a lot of blood during the delivery. But soon we were all home together, and he grew to be one chubby baby that my father called "Churchill", in an affectionate way of course. More on my son later.

> "'Lo, children are an heritage of the Lord: and the fruit of the womb is his reward' (King James Version, Ps. 127.3)."

I remember when our son was about six months old he had a little romper that was turquoise and lime green. I liked the colors so much that my husband agreed to paint our living room in those exact shades. It really turned out very lovely. Another time we painted a couple of walls orange, and then the remaining walls we put up white paneling. Everything we decorated together looked nice. One of the memories I have during those times is how I would often sit on the floor and we would talk to each other as he painted. That is an extremely fond memory. We enjoyed talking with each other. There were also times we argued, or rather I should say I argued. He remained calm and I was always the one who ended up feeling guilty. Something never felt right about that. It works better, I think, when both people are involved in a conversation, argument or not. I don't know if this is right, or not.

Here is something comical about living in our home. We were always moving rooms around! First our living room was just that, a living room. Then because our kitchen was too small to have company dinners, we moved our living room to the basement and paneled those walls. When our son came along and got old enough for his own room, we also moved our bedroom down in the basement and put up a dividing wall of panel to separate it from the living room. Then we moved our daughter into what used to be our bedroom, so each of our children could have their own room. The flowered wallpaper was traded in for fire engines. It is a wonder anybody knew which room was which! Are you completely confused by now?!

16
I Think, I Feel; Who Cares?

When I first began seeing the counselor I used a lot of "I think" statements. Even though I was a very feeling person, it seemed safer to think. One day he said he was tired of hearing me say "I think", and wanted to know what I felt. And pretty soon I was writing many poems that told how I felt. And gradually the feelings spilled out and overflowed. There were so many times I felt overwhelmed. I don't think anyone ever asked me before how, or what I was feeling. Can you imagine that? Can you relate to that? In my family growing up, we all just did what needed to be done, and didn't sit down ever and share feelings. I remember one time my dad was upset with me at something I said to him. He got mad at me and I had a look on my face that he didn't like. He told me, "Wipe that look off your face!" Later when I apologized, he couldn't accept my apology. Any feelings I had I pretty much kept to myself, at least the majority of time.

AUGUST 10, 1971

Come Out
I want to come out of myself –
Out of my prison of fear,
Of false safety –
But only I can use the key to set me free.

There are constant reminders ever before me of
freedom:
Freedom to love, freedom to care, freedom to feel,
freedom to express the feelings that give life
meaning.

There is peace in accepting one's self,
For it leads to accepting life,

And in accepting life, the ability to accept others.

Oh, God! I want to come out of this prison of fear.
Help me to find the key,
And to set myself free.

Yes, I lived inside myself, often. On the outside I seemed like I had everything in control; on the inside I was always afraid. I would catch myself walking around sighing deeply, or find that my hands were clenched in a fist. I was often talking not only to the Lord, but to myself, and to the counselor, who wasn't even present. My mind was constantly on overdrive, working on problems, and working on myself. I had worn a mask for so long that it became natural to show others what I felt safe in showing them. It also helped me cope with my fear; at least I thought it did. But I had such a desire to be free; to be on the inside what people saw on the outside. In many some ways, I was the same; but the fear, anger, and torment I felt, I kept pretty much to myself. And it was those emotions that made me feel like a fake, and ugly. Sometimes on Sunday mornings when I would be getting ready for church, I would look in the mirror and say to myself, "People think you are so sweet, but if they really knew you, they wouldn't think that." I wanted to be sweet all the time. I wanted to have patience all the time. I wanted to know the Lord was pleased with me all the time. I wanted to feel okay.

And I couldn't feel okay because I lived with mistrust, fear, and anger much of the time, and had no way to control it, nor the circumstances which created it.

"'Bring my soul out of prison, that I may praise Thy name' (King James Version, Ps. 142.7)."

This, of course, was not really prison, but rather a feeling of being all bound up inside. It felt like prison to me.
The Lord, is so Amazing. He is so Patient. He is so Understanding. He waits, and He walks with us, sight unseen.

I was so in need of having a safe place to come to, a safe person to be with, that the psychologist became a leaning post, like a giant tree. I valued the wisdom and discernment he had, and he spent many hours, and years listening, and counseling. He was someone who really cared about the pain we were in.

My husband and I spent literally a fortune for this counsel. I rather regret spending all that money because he was unable to save the marriage; but then neither could God, though He wanted to. It was our God-given free will that prevented our successful marriage, not the Lord's desire.

We all have the responsibility in life to live and obey Him, and when we don't He does not always protect us from the consequences.

NOVEMBER 8, 1971

The Counselor
I met a man today - a lover of himself,
A lover of men, a lover of God, a searcher of hearts.
Today I met a man.

I met a man today while buried 'neath my fear
And, though I struggled and fought self,
Though I hated, and though I hurt and covered me
up,
He looked for me
So gently, and I let him find me.
Today I met a man.

I met a man today and dearer to my heart he grew.
He drew me close and again I struggled,
And once again I fought, and again I feared.

Still he held me, and at last I knew I was safe,
And I trusted.
Today, I met a man.

The counselor was the first man in my life who unselfishly cared about what I felt. I was overwhelmed and I just kept cranking poem after poem out in an attempt to be heard and understood. Looking back over the poem above I am reminded that it is unwise to depend too heavily on any one person. We must, however, remember that the Lord is a jealous God. He is jealous for our good. We are not to make anyone, or anything an idol.

November 11, 1971

Silver Tray
I have my heart on a silver tray,
Bare for all to see.
It's lying here, searching everywhere,
Crying out, "Please love me."

Doesn't anyone know I'm lonely?
Can't anyone hear me cry?
I want to be loved for me only,
Yet all of you pass me by.

Hey you! Hey mister! I'm growing tired and cold,
And you're my last chance, I'm told.
Won't you please love me today?
I'll give you my heart on this silver tray.

November 11, 1971

The Caring of a Heart
I've never given away my heart,
Never even wanted to, Until now;
And now, I give it to you.

I hope that you will take it,
You've taken others before,
And cared for them so tenderly,
Never dropped them to the floor.

I know you'll never trample it,
Or throw it carelessly down;
For you don't treat hearts that way,
You carry them gently around.

I'm glad I'm giving you my heart,

For in giving, I receive,
A freedom to love, A freedom to care,
A freedom my heart with others to share.

My heart had been stomped on, torn apart, and ripped to shreds over and over again, and now the counselor was someone who finally valued it.

There are people everywhere, that we see every day, who are crying out in the same way. My children, my own children, be on the lookout for them. Reach out to them. They are in all walks of life. They dress, and speak, and act in all sorts of ways in order to cover up their pain. Someone(s) needs you. Someone needs the hope that only Jesus can give. He wants to use you as His instrument of love. But be careful, be honorable, be trustworthy, and pray for wisdom when someone hurting comes to you. That is the way Jesus is.

"'Men groan from out of the city, and the soul of the wounded crieth out' (King James Version, Job 24.12)."

Oh my, yes. Yes, this is true.

1971-1972   Separation
Sometime between 1971 and 1972 the counselor suggested a six-month separation. This was the first one. We were physically separated, but talked regularly on the phone. I have no idea if this was wise or not; it certainly kept us connected. Our daughter would have been about six at this time. She said she would wash the dishes every night if we would stay together. Have you ever heard of anything so sweet, and so sad at the same time.

FEBRUARY 7, 1972
While watching our two-year-old son playing at my feet as I sat knitting; here is what I thought:

My Little Boy
He's sitting here before my eyes;
my son, at two,
a soul so beautiful.

I remember as I looked at him and saw the innocence of this little boy, I thought what a gift the Lord blessed me with. I could go back to that house today, and sit in that same spot, and say to myself, "what a gift." I am so proud of my son. He is a creative thinker, and one who is gifted to serve others. He is a musician with a beautiful voice, and an accomplished pianist, and has written several pieces of music. He is also accomplished in the field of administration. He and his wife are building their own generation to follow Him, in my grandson. My son is a wonderful father, teaching my grandson the scriptures and principles to help him lead a Godly life. He is kind, self-effacing, and a man after God's heart. He is resolved and committed to his family. He is a hard worker, but he is often too intense. He is overcoming tremendous obstacles in his life. He is a warrior's Warrior. As I previously said, his name means "peace". Yes, the two can go hand-in-hand.

"'But as for me and my house, we will serve the Lord' (King James Version, Josh. 24.15b)."

Most people are looking, sometimes unknowingly for a person they can share their inner most feelings with. Often we are less than comfortable with the feelings of others, and many times are careless with them, so people become fearful of sharing their hopes, their hurts, and their hearts. Jesus can always be trusted.

APRIL 23, 1972

Valued
Give me your feelings
And I'll carefully hold them;
Please leave me be a part of you,
And in return, I will share me.

JUNE 26, 1972

Revealed
Revealed.

My heart has willingly, fearfully revealed itself to you.

Revealed.

My heart is warmer now than it was before when it was all bundled up.

Amazing!

Revealed.

My heart, come out of hiding and you will reward yourself.

17

Desert Storms

FEBRUARY 1976   I am 35. Birthday surprise.

I was reading the morning paper and saw my husband's name and our address. This was the way I found out that my husband was again in trouble with the law. At the time I was preparing to have a birthday party for our son. Inside I was so scared, and my nerves felt like they were jumping out of my skin. This was not the time to fall apart, so the party went on. I honestly just did not know what else to do. When I had a chance I called the counselor. Before that, I just pretended that everything was okay. Even today I see myself frozen at the sink trying to comprehend. You would think that by this time I would not suffer such shock. I frequently was suspicious, and yet at the same time, always trying to convince myself that I was wrong in my suspicions. I was in a constant battle. Yet when something overt happened I went into shock, and overdrive trying to make things as normal as possible. I could not allow my children to find out about these incidents. I had to keep everything going for all of us.

Following this incident, my husband was placed on probation. I remember the trips to the probation office with him. The lawyer believed it would help my husband if I showed my support by going along. The fact that he was in counseling helped his case also. This probation was for a year and there were no other known incidents during this time. Following this year the counselor suggested we separate once again, this time for 18 months; thinking, hoping that this might help the marriage to survive. This was our second separation. Our daughter was 11, and our son just turned 6. Always during our separations, which was hard on our children, we would tell them that "mommy and daddy are having problems, and need to be apart for a while". I doubt this made it much easier for them but at least they did not have to choose sides. They went to their father's apartment every other weekend to spend time with him. I believed this was the right thing to do. I have my doubts that it was.

I would encourage you parents now that if you and your spouse are having serious issues, or even small problems, be careful that you don't blame one another to your small children. It isn't necessary, nor helpful to them. But I am sure that it was not healthy to cover things up to the degree I did. No easy answer.

Again I will say, "we are each responsible for our own actions." God wants so much to help each of us to grow beyond the lies we often believe about ourselves, and the destructive thinking and actions those beliefs can cause.

It may be hard for some of you to understand that in between all the trauma we thoroughly enjoyed being with each other. We had fun together; we talked of spiritual things; we planned; and we worked at making a life together. We went to church regularly. We had friends who often came to our home for dinner and a time of fellowship. Strange, I know, but that is what living in denial can do. It was how we coped with an awful problem. And there was always hope. Hope is a wonderful, God-given gift, but it needs to be based on reality, or it can make room for hopeless. But then I don't believe in hopeless, nor do I believe God does either.

"'But for him who is joined to all the living, there is hope' (King James Version, Eccles. 9.4a)."

Be assured, there is hope, and there is The Hope, for you too.

1976   It seems a bit odd to me that the next poem makes its way here at this time. It does however provide a welcome relief in the midst of all the serious writing.

When I was a little girl my Grandparents Zarfoss had a cherry wood rocking chair. As I rocked and rocked on it I would find myself in another part of the room from where I had started. The memory of that is as real today as it was when I wrote this next poem.

Grandma's Rocking Chair
I wish I had a rocking chair
Like Grandma's long ago;
With pillows all around me
I'd rock back to and fro.

I'd start out in one corner,
The way I used to do,
And then before I'd know it
I'd be across the room!

Perhaps I'd sit on someone's lap,
Pretend that I was wee
Maybe I would take a nap
And dream on endlessly.

Yes, I'd dream on endlessly.

The squeaks, they wouldn't bother me,
So steady they would be –
Like raindrops on the roof at night,
We'd listen quietly.

C'mon, close your eyes and dream with me
Of Grandma's long ago;
We'll draw upon sweet memories
As we rock, to and fro.

18
Songs in the Night

APRIL 1976   I turn 45.   Another birthday surprise.
Much to my surprise one day a large truck pulled up outside
the house, and two men began hauling a piano up the side walk to the
front door. This was in 1976, and it was my birthday. It was a gift my
husband had delivered. Though we were separated we were on good
terms, and tried to keep our problems from our children. They would
visit him on weekends, and he and I talked on the phone on almost a
daily basis. Still, I was not prepared for a gift. Gifts during a separation
can really confuse the emotions. The giver can feel good, and the
receiver can feel guilty, and bought.
It was during the first week of having the piano that I decided
to try my hand at writing music. That became the second gift. I had
never written music before. Even in hard times the Lord gives good
gifts. Sometimes, especially during the hard times. Perhaps it is a type
of balm. I've included the words to the songs that I've written.

"'God, my maker, gives songs in the night' (King
James Version, Job 35.10)."

APRIL 1976   Written for a nurse friend who was going
through a rough time, and needed someone to listen to her. Following
lunch with her, I wrote this song.

Listen to Me
I came to see you aching inside,
Will you please listen, be on my side?
I need no lectures, just want to be
Sitting with someone who cares for me.

Chorus
Won't you please listen to me, listen to me,

Spend some time with me,
Listen to me, listen to me,
I'm in need, you see.

You gave me coffee, you gave me time,
You placed your quiet heart next to mine.
I feel more peaceful, rested and clear,
For you have listened and you stayed near.

APRIL 1976   Written about a man struggling with mental
problems, and behaving poorly. Mark 5 was used as a reference. Lest
you think this was in reference to my husband, it was not.

I Know A Man
I know a man, so lost and broken,
He's struggling in his misery;
He's sick, and mean, and Oh so helpless,
And drowning in his own dark sea.

But the lame were made to walk,
And the blind were made to see,
And miracles still happen,
O Love reach in and set him free.

And Love reached in and set him free.
And then He told him to go,
And tell all the people
That the Lord had made him whole.

APRIL 1976   This next song is one of my favorites; it has
a very haunting melody. This is also my daughter's favorite.

Song of the Soul
My soul sings, but not in harmony;
My heart beats in awkward time;
And hopes sore with dreams that are off key,
While my feet walk a wayward line.
Life starts with cries of agony,
And days end so much the same,

The space between we search on endlessly
For a purpose so few have gained.

There's beauty the human eye can see,
And beauty we'll never know.
What's the point of earth, the stars, the sky, the sea,
And why is real love so hard to show?

And why am I here?
I do not know.

"'Turn thee unto me, and have mercy upon me; for I
am desolate and afflicted. The troubles of my heart
are enlarged: O bring thou me out of my distresses'
(King James Version, Ps. 25.16-17)."

One Sunday morning the pastor spoke about the apostle Paul
being in chains, and in prison. He was chained because of his love for
Christ, and the people. I thought this would be a good song for little
children to sing. I could picture them standing in a circle, holding
hands, and pretending that each one was a link in a chain.

APRIL 1976

Love Links
Jesus is our love link to the Father above;
Jesus, our example, to be a link of love.

I am a link, A link in a chain;
A chain that belongs to the Lord.
You are a link, A link in a chain;
A chain that belongs to the Lord.

You're a love link to your daddy,
A love link to your friend;
A love link to your mother,
And to the one next door.

A love link to your brother,

That's what God needs you for;
Will you be a love link?
He wants many more.

Some links are loyal,
Some are beautiful;
Some links are strong,
Some dependable

Some links are rusty,
Some are broken too,
None of them are perfect,
So there's a place for me and you.

Here is another one which would be great for preschoolers in Bible School. It is sung to the tune of "Row, row, row your boat". Are you familiar with this true event in the Old Testament of Moses leading the children of Israel through the Red Sea, parted by the hand of God? It can be found in Exodus chapter 14.

Get Ready to March
March, march, march along
March toward the sea;
God will guide and protect us
From the enemy.

March, march, march along
Together you and me;
Follow the Guide and be on His side
As we march toward the sea.

Look! Look! there is the sea;
God has made a way To escape the enemy,
Trust Him and obey.

April 1976

A Child's Need
We need our father to show us love

Like our heavenly Father up above.
We need our father to clothe and feed us,
Hug and teach us, how to grow.

Chorus
Daddy, I love you; Daddy, will you be true to me
Daddy, I need you To help me grow.

We need our mommy to show us love
Like our heavenly Father up above
We need our mommy to laugh and cry with,
Hug and teach us how to grow.

Chorus
Mommy, I love you; Mommy, will you be true to me,
Mommy, I need you To help me grow.

I was recently sharing with my daughter-in-law how even
after a child is disciplined how quickly they are to love again; they
don't hold a grudge. I wonder when that changes. It often seems that
a child is the one who best exemplifies the teaching in Matthew
chapter 18 where the Lord tells us to forgive over and over again.

MAY 24, 1976

Alone
Do you feel like you missed the boat today?
Are you sitting alone on the shore?
Does it seem your friends have all found God's way?
And you're more alone than before?

You find no hope in what people say,
They are not struggling like you;
You see their joy as they pass your way
On a boat that is sailing by too.

But you smile and wave with an unseen sigh,
So they can't see how your heart aches.
They can't understand the tears in your eyes,

Nor the reason your foolish heart breaks.

Are you burdened by the Lord's command
To be joyful all the day through?
Does it seem that He's never satisfied?
Always asking more from you.

It is not hard to see I was feeling depressed.

MAY 25, 1976

In A Dream
I stood on a hill last night
With people all around;
My eyes took in a glorious sight
When I saw the Lord coming down.

The clouds did part for Him;
I shouted "Here He comes";
His robe was white, His arms were wide;
I knew He'd come for some.

My eyes held fast, I could not move,
The presence of others grew dim;
My heart was faint, I waited in fear;
O would He let me in?

And then I awoke and knew,
That I had seen a dream;
I pondered what took place last night
When I stood on the hill with Him.

And I continued to write music all that year. This next one
came as a result of feelings I was having while sitting in church on a
particular Sunday

God Has Noticed You
One Sunday morning while in church,
Some people took a part;

I sat back on the sidelines
With questions in my heart.

I felt nobody noticed me,
And I began to churn;
When I came home I wrote this song,
And here is what I learned.

Some folks are easily noticed,
They're witty or their gay;
They're beautiful or boisterous
As they travel on their way.

They're cunning or creative,
Talents not a few;
They're smiling, happy, friendly folks,
But they don't notice you.

You can't do anything special,
You say this to yourself;
You can't do anything really well,
So you place your gifts on a shelf;

You don't contribute what you have,
You're busy being shy;
So folks will never notice you,
They'll just pass you by.

C'mon and face the problem,
You fear you'll come in last;
You're busy with comparisons
Instead of with the task;

You're scared you won't do better than
The folks surrounding you;
And then you'll feel all hurt inside
'Cause they didn't notice you.

You have a lot to offer,

It's right there in your heart;
A smile, an ear, a helping hand;
Please come and share a part

Of you, and talents that you have;
Stop fearing what you'll do,
If friendly, busy, happy folks
Shouldn't notice you.

Stop fearing what you'll do;
For God has noticed you!

JUNE 17, 2017   It is interesting that just last evening I was feeling overlooked when I wanted to share a particular talent, and was not immediately given affirmation. This morning as I was reading my Bible the Lord spoke to my heart as I read this verse in Proverbs:

"'A fool has no delight in understanding, but in expressing his own heart' (New King James Version, Prov. 18.2)."

I thought to myself that I must be patient, and accept the possibility that my time for wanting to do such and such might not be God's time. This has put my heart at ease so that I do not become resentful.

JULY 12, 1976

Hidden Dream
Do you have a dream that lives in your heart;
A dream that few people share?
I know about dreams that live in the heart,
For I, too, have one living there.

My dream can warm me when I'm cold inside.
My dream is comforting and dear.
So tender when I'm feeling old inside;
My dream is someone always near.

Can you run off to the dream in your heart;
Can you stop and rest for a while;
Then get up refreshed, and begin a new start-
Can you look at yourself, and smile?

My dream can raise me when I've fallen down,
And awake with me each time I call,
With arms about me when I'm full of fear;
And though alone, I'm not alone at all.

"My God is an Artist" came to me as I was taking a walk in the fall of 1976. The leaves on the trees were all turning the most vibrant colors. It was a gorgeous scene!

SEPTEMBER 1976

My God Is An Artist
As I was walking down the street one day,
I looked up into the sky.
I saw the lovely whites on blue
As they went drifting by.

I then looked down upon the ground
And saw the brightness of green,
With yellow and reds in flower beds,
I so enjoyed the scene.

Chorus
My God is an artist, He puts colors all around;
The silver in a raindrop as it falls upon the ground;
The orange and yellow of the leaves on trees as fall
comes rolling around;
The pink and white as a snowflake as winter comes
to town.

I realized the Lord delighted
In these colors too.
He loves to paint and re-create,
And gaze upon us too.

I felt we shared a common pleasure
On that beautiful day, And I could understand Him in
a new and different way.

Chorus
My God is an artist for He painted me and you;
Some of us are yellow, some are red, or brown,
some like a snowflake too.
Some eyes are green and some are brown, some as
the sky of blue.
And lovelier then gold our worth I'm told, Is His
creation too.

SEPTEMBER 9, 1976

His Love For Me
I just saw a glimpse of Jesus' love
For me, for me.
While on my knees, feeling angry with Him,
He gave this gift to me.

Such a tiny glimpse of God's love,
But it meant so much to me;
For He met me there in my heart of despair,
And He gave of Himself for me.

Chorus
His love for me, His love for me,
So much greater than I can see.
His love for me, His love for me,
I saw a glimpse of God's love for me.

My heart wonders at Jesus love;
He decided for me long ago.
Now hungry I feel, with a yearning inside,
For more of His love to know.

He has such a different love;
He gives His life to me.

He will not move, never turn away,
And He steadily gives,
He readily gives His love.

SEPTEMBER 14, 1976   In my Bible, I wrote, "A new beginning." I wrote the same thing a few months later, and don't remember why I wrote it either time. It is interesting to me that both of these statements are written when I was reading the beginning of Romans chapter 13 in the Living New Translation.

NOVEMBER 3, 1976   I found written in the Living New Translation section of my Parallel Bible this verse, and my comment:

"'Your old evil desires were nailed to the cross with Him; that part of you that loves to sin was crushed and fatally wounded, so that your sin-loving nature is no longer under sin's control, no longer needs to be a slave to sin' (Living New Translation, Rom. 6.6)."

NOVEMBER 7, 1976   I feel so unbearably lonely.

1977

Solace
I want to rest in the arms of God tonight.
I want to look at His face so filled with love.
Where no harm befalls me,
And no darkness calls me.
And so to rest in the arms of God tonight.

This next song I wrote after the death of Grandfather Coldren. It is very sad to think this is the way I felt. Each soul is very precious to God, and He is never wanting anyone leave this life without Him.

FEBRUARY 12, 1977

Without Jesus
A man died today without the Savior;

My heart was cold, I did not care.
What makes me filled with such contentment?
While people are passing away?

Chorus
Without Jesus, I would have no hope;
Without Jesus, I'd die in my sin;
And live forever removed from the presence of God,
Without Jesus, my Savior.

FEBRUARY 22, 1977   This song, too, has a very haunting melody;
just picture this lamb. Are you waiting for this wonderful Loving
Shepherd? He is waiting for you to come to Him. This is one of my
son's favorites; I wrote it ten days after he turned seven.

Little Lamb
There was a lamb alone on the highway of life;
All alone, so alone, waiting there.
As the lamb looked around at the hard, stony
ground,
To the blue of the sky over head.

She grew patient and smiled, for she knew He would
come,
And the Lord, He was already there.
Yes, the Lord, He was already there.

Shepherd, speak to your lamb, Shepherd, here is my
hand,
As He looked, as He spoke of Himself.
"Little lamb, follow Me, I am gentle, and meek; and I
love you, yes, I love you, little lamb"
And He loves you, yes, He loves you little lamb.

"'Woe to the idle shepherd that leaveth the flock'
(King James Version, Zech. 11.17)."

Jesus is the Shepherd that will never leave, nor abandon His
flock. Jesus says in John's gospel.

"I am the good Shepherd: the good Shepherd giveth
his life for the sheep... I am the good Shepherd, and
know my sheep, and am known of mine' (King James
Version, John 10.11; 10.14)

Take time and read about the Shepherd in Ezekiel 34, please
do.

SEPTEMBER 1977   This next song is a curiosity because I have forgotten
the melody. Some of the songs above I have the music actually written
on staff paper, and some are only in my head. This particular one I
have neither, only the words.

Song Without A Melody
Sometimes we get caught up
In the pride of being right,
And we pull at those around us
To do all things our way.

One day we discover
Our rightness has been wrong,
And we must re-examine our heart.

There is only one who is always right;
Jesus, our Lord.
He is our Teacher, He gives us strength
To follow the better way of love.

If all we can see is the mote in our brother's eye,
If all we can see is what's wrong with him,
If we can't acknowledge the beam that is blinding us,
It's time to re-examine our heart.

Chorus
Love doesn't demand its own way,
love is patient and kind.
Love will correct us, encourage and strengthen us
To follow His better way.

OCTOBER 1977

For Me
The Father gave His son, the Savior of men,
No words can describe the Love He has given;
A gentle man with a holy mission,
Seeking not His own life, But our salvation.

Chorus
When He hung there on the tree, He knew me;
He knew my name, He bore the shame
Of one not yet born, When He gave His life for me.

There are no words to describe the Savior of men,
No words to describe the love He has given;
He left his home, and His glory above,
Became our Redeemer to demonstrate God's love.

NOVEMBER 6, 1977

Who Is He?
He tenderly turned my heart,
He planted the seed of love,
He silently made a change in me
When He tenderly my turned heart.

He freely forgives my past,
He buries it and forgets,
And when I sin, I'm free to ask For He settled,
forgave my past.

Chorus
Who is He? Who is this?
Who's that One? Jesus, the Lord.
He calls me to follow Him.
The way is sometimes unknown.

As we walk,
He tells of His promise true,

Never to leave me alone.

He lovingly lifts me up,
I'm wayward and sometimes I fall.
He patiently waits to strengthen me
He knows my voice when I call.

Following these 18 songs, I did not write for the next three years. It is interesting to me how that gift of the piano sparked something in me I didn't realize I had. The Lord is the giver of all good gifts, and also good at surprising us!

If you remember the Lord used my mother to give me a book of poetry which watered the seed of poetry in me, and next He used my estranged husband, during a separation to give me a piano, which planted the seed of writing music in me.

"Every good gift and perfect gift is from above, and cometh down from the Father of lights, with whom is no variableness neither shadow of turning' (King James Version, Jas. 1.17)."

He is sometimes quietly Amazing!

19
My Mother's New Home

JANUARY 29,1978   I am 46. My husband and I are back together.

We sell our house and are moving into a home that is being built. It was to be ready by February of 1979. I remember the enjoyment we had in picking out the carpets, new furniture, paint colors, etc. My mother had suggested a tiffany lamp for our dining room, which we purchased. It is sad that she never got to see it, or the inside of our lovely new home. I did drive by with her and she got to see the outside. This was in January 1979. She died on January 24. (We moved the following month.) She entered her eternal home a month before we moved to our new earthly home. Who do you think got the best deal? And SOMEONE ELSE paid for hers!

In February of the previous year my mother was diagnosed with lymphoma. She was 57. I remember combing her hair for her one day and it was coming out in clumps in my hand. I also remember she was happy that my husband and I were back together. I'm sure she was concerned about me spending my life alone, and while my parents knew about our problems, I protected them from the full extent as long as I could. She never lived long enough to be part of the sad and catastrophic end of our marriage. I'm glad.

I was the last person to see her on the night she died. When I entered her hospital room she was sleeping, and I sat there until she woke up. When she woke up she wondered why I didn't wake her up. She told me she could sleep anytime.

I sat on her bed and we talked. She talked about some of her personal things like her engagement ring, her mother's ring, and a fur coat, and who she wanted to have them. I didn't want to talk about that, but she said it gave her something to think about as she lay there. She was so, so sick. She told my dad she didn't want any visitors that night, but as my family and I were eating dinner, I told my husband I just had to go to see her. I believe that was the way God led me, for it was our last time together.

I was the last person to see her. At eight o'clock visiting hours were over. I wish I would have insisted on staying, but I was a rule follower, and obediently left. Today I would do differently. Before going, my mother and I told one another we loved each other. Then I left. She died around 11 o'clock that night.

I wish I could tell her again that I love her. I love you, Mother".

I wrote the poem "Soon" between the time I left the hospital and the time she died, and yet I don't remember thinking she was going to die. When I got the news that night about midnight, I remember sobbing and saying, "Not yet, not yet". I left and went to my parent's place to be with my dad. That is when he said, "It should have been me". He felt so bad for the years he smoked, and blamed himself. That was such an awful time for us; and then he and I had to go shopping to buy something for her to wear.

JANUARY 24, 1979

Soon
Soon she'll be with Him - soon she'll see His face.
The pain will be gone and she'll be in His eyes.
Oh Lord, our Hope, Almighty Lover and Healer
How You want to comfort us!

Just because we know our loved ones have gone to be with the Lord, we do not want to pretend it doesn't hurt to no longer have them with us. It can be very painful to realize we will not see or hear their voice again here on earth. When my mother died I would find myself crying at unexpected moments for a full year. One of the many things I remembered about her was how whenever she came to visit she would always compliment me on how pretty things looked. She always noticed if I had rearranged the furniture, or had a new item sitting around. I missed that she would never walk through our door again. She often called me "Honey".

But there was one time I got a scolding! We had just recently gotten a new automatic washing machine, and my mother went to take some wash out of it for me. I had not kept it very clean on top, and she said, "I don't ever want to see your washer looking like this again!" And it never did. I still remember that scolding some 50 years later!

With all the sadness we feel when a loved one dies, we do have this eternal hope found in the verses which follow.

> "'So shall we [she] I ever be with the Lord' (King James Version, 1 Thess. 4.17)."

I read Psalm 91 the night my mother died. The first verse was a comfort to me.

> "'He that dwelleth in the secret place of the most High shall abide under the shadow of the Almighty' (King James Version, Ps. 91.1)."

> "'To everything there is a season, a time to every purpose under the heaven: A time to be born, and a time to die' (King James Version, Eccles. 3.1-2)."

I will see her, and my father one day.

20
On the Road Again

Six months later we were on the move again. This time it was because two weeks after we moved into our new house, there was a major crisis at Three-Mile Island, and I was afraid this would cause us health problems. So we decided to move from that house and buy one about 15 miles away. We settled in and began decorating and fixing up this one. As before, it was fun. I do wonder, in retrospect, if we moved so much because it gave us the illusion that life was changing for the better. I'm not sure.

It was 1979, and this was the last home we bought together. I was so hopeful that things would work out. We were together until 1984.

God's enemy is seeking to destroy God's families.

It might be noted here that from 1979 until 1984 I did not write any poetry, with the exception of a poem about the six days of Creation, for that year's vacation Bible school.

1980

The Six Days of Creation
On the first day of creation
The Lord God turned on the Light.
He separated the darkness,
And now we have day and night.

On the second day of creation
The Lord God formed the heavens
Water below, He said and it was so

Was He done? No, His work had just begun.

Now day three, The land and sea;

Grass and seeds, and flowering trees
What a beautiful sight to see!

What was on day four? Can there be more?

Heavenly sunshine, heavenly sunshine,
Stars and moon for seasons and time.
And He said "It is good".

On day number five
All the fish and the birds came alive;
Great, great whales with long, long tails;
And He blessed them, He multiplied them.

And He said "It is good".

On the sixth day of creation
Our animal friends were made;
And then God said, "Let Us make man!"
And it was good!

Now God could rest. He finished what He planned.
He looked all around, from the sky to the ground,
And He said, "It is good, It is good."
It is grand!

I did however write some more music. After hearing a lesson in Sunday School, the words for this song came to me. It was followed by two more.

1980

Sin-Debt Paid
I stood before the Father, The Holy God above;
He asked me why He should let me in.
My heart began pounding, and I felt so afraid,
But I remembered my sin debt was paid

Chorus

When I saw Jesus, Jesus, standing by me,
Bearing the sin that God laid on Him,
Now I no longer need be afraid
Because Jesus, my penalty paid.

My Father looked at me, But right past my sin;
He opened His arms, And He drew us within;
My Savior beside me and I no longer afraid;
So thankful my sin debt He paid.

Chorus
And I said Jesus, Jesus, how you loved me;
You carried my sin so that I could go free;
Because of You, I stand here today
Because Jesus, my penalty you paid.

This next song was written for a family reunion. We all sat around a long dinner table; there were many of us, and we sang it together. This was my husband's family. They were each blessed with lovely voices, able to blend together. Since that time three of our family members have gone to heaven. One, my children's father, and the other two, their grandfather, and grandmother, plus my own mother and father, and other family members as well.

A person can never be replaced. We sometimes don't realize this until they are no longer with us.

In 2016 this same song, with only a very few minor changes was sung by our Ladies Missionary Fellowship, for the luncheon. It was my honor to be able to play for them, and hear it sung. A family, and a church family, bear many similarities.

1981

A Family Song
As we gather here together
one by one to share family fun,
Let us now join hands and remember
God, our Father, Christ, His Son.

Chorus

Let us thank God together for each one,
Let us thank Him together for His Son;
Let us join now in singing a sweet song,
And rejoice with each other in His holy word.

To the left and to the right
we know each one by name;
And when one of us is missing,
it isn't quite the same;

Bridge
Meeting a need in the family of God;
Lending a hand, is part of the plan.
Bearing a burden and sharing a care
Is how we show God's love 'round here.

21
New Plans

1982   My husband and I decided to start our own
business. We were both excited, and turned our former family room
into an office. I was his secretary. He was to do the manual labor. We
bought a van, and put the name of the company on the side, along
with the following scripture verse

> "'In all labor there is profit, but idle chatter lead only
> to poverty' (King James Version, Prov. 14.23)."

This was a good verse to use because my husband was a hard laborer.
My job was pretty easy. I had only to keep the books, answer the
phone, and set up return phone calls. We were up and running.

JANUARY 13, 1983   For some reason I no longer remember, I
kept a small square piece of red paper that my husband wrote the
following on. I am inserting it here merely to show that these were the
things that were on his mind on this particular day.

A day of decision and crisis

1. *Withdraw from union as an act of faith.*
2. *Arranging a conference with Jeff's gym
   teacher as an act of love.*
3. *Student aid for Melody's school (Eastern)*
4. *Possibly sending Jeff to Christian school next
   year.*
5. *Haven't had much work; Lord's guidance
   and supplying needs.*
6. *Me to be more sensitive to Jeff*

1983   I've often wondered what Jesus looked like as a child; what kind of interests he had; and what kind of personality. We know He was perfect, but I would have liked to have known Him then. This curiosity prompted me to write a song imagining what He might have been like from childhood to the end of His earthly life. The Bible doesn't give us a whole lot of detail about Him when He was a child and adolescent. It focuses on His purpose for coming to earth, which was to die for the sins of the world.

From a Boy to a Man; This Man Jesus
A baby boy was born one day,
Willingly He came;
He had a purpose and a plan,
He even had a name.

He left His home familiar a
And said, "Farewell, My God",
And allowed Himself to be lowered
To earth's cold sod.

Chorus
My God, what a wondrous Gift You gave,
Dear Lord, did you ever feel alone?
Leaving the sweet security
Of Your Father and Your home.

A small child began growing,
Was it very hard my Lord?
Were you then all-knowing,
and did you ever feel bored?

Did you miss Your Father, God;
Were you always aware
Of His being right within You,
And His Fatherly care?

Soon you came to teen years,
Did you have any fun?
Were you always mindful

Of the need to be done.

Were you then concerned
With souls lost in sin?
And did you know at that time, Lord
That You were the only way in?

Did You ever think of marriage,
Were You ever in love
With anyone but Your Father,
And Your home above?

Many must have loved You
For the kindness you'd shown,
Did you ever fall in love Lord,
But decide to live alone?

As You carried Your cross that day, Lord.
After all the love you'd shown;
How did you stand the pain Lord,
Of being all alone?

No one else was able
In your place to stand,
You alone could die
For the sin of every man.

Chorus
My God, what a wondrous Gift You gave
To free Your loved ones from the fall;
You kept the promise You alone had made;
You gave Your heart, Your Son, Your all.

Here comes the Bride Sin for atoned;
Jesus sought and bought us
We're on our way home.

I doubt that any of us can accurately imagine what our perfect home, our eternal home, will be like. But we know Jesus is building one for us. Can you imagine that!

> "'In My Father's house are many mansions; if it were not so I would have told you. I go to prepare a place for you' (New King James Version, John 14.2)."

1984   We are now planning a wedding for our 19-year-old daughter. After attending college for a year, she decided it wasn't for her. She and her fiancé decided to get married, and they set the date for December. It was around this time that my husband took her fiancé on as an apprentice in his work. Things in our life seemed to be going well. There was much planning to be done. We made a guest list, and ordered the napkins with their names and date on. The attendants were chosen, and we began to talk about flowers. It was a busy time, but an enjoyable one. It was to be a rather large, and lovely wedding.

Even though in many respects I led a busy enough life with office work, knitting, crocheting, appointments, and planning a wedding, I sometimes still felt dissatisfied inside. I felt there was a part of me that wanted to do more creative things, and I already was doing quite a few. On this particular day I put these feelings into a poem.

MAY 1984

Dissatisfied
The Lord is working through my discontent
As I look at how my days are spent:
The TV on at break of day
Before I even think to pray.

I've learned to covet my days alone,
Safely wrapped inside my home,
For I'm not one to over commit,
And so within these walls I sit.

Something is missing - or needs added on.
I've something to offer before my life is gone.

Growing up I remember hearing people complain because they agreed to take on a task or position that they really didn't want. Because of that I decided I would not fall into that trap. I would only agree to do things I really wanted to do.

Because of this I found it easier to say "No" than "Yes". It was less scary then to commit to something that I may at some point want to get out of. I think because of that decision, I sometimes missed opportunities afforded me.

22
Screams in the Desert

August 1984   I am 43. There is that dreadful knock.
While our daughter was out with her fiancé, my husband and I were in our room when there was a knock at the door. I answered it. There were two policemen standing there; they had come for my husband. I remember I cowered behind the door shaking and crying silently as I tried to grasp what was happening. The feeling that he had done something wrong was all too familiar. I stood there in my pink robe and listened to the police ask me if my husband was home, and tell me they needed to speak with him. I remember how concerned and kind they were to me, asking me if I was alright. They could tell I wasn't, but I think they just didn't know what to say. They were there to do a job, a painful one. I was concerned our son might be aware of what was going on because he was in his nearby bedroom, so I gathered my emotions together and went back the hall and motioned for my husband to come. As we were walking down the hall I whispered to him that the police were at the door for him. He said, "I didn't do anything, Barb, honest I didn't do anything". But he did. They took him to their car in hand cuffs.

After they left, I went out to the office, closed the door, and called my husband's mother. As you can imagine we were both very upset. She felt worse for me, I think, than my husband. You see, she had been through similar circumstances in her life. She understood. I do remember I was laying on the floor, behind the desk, with the phone, and being as quiet as I could be so my son wouldn't hear me crying. One of the things I told my mother-in-law was that I would stick by my husband. I remember her saying, "That is beautiful". At the time I guess that was in my heart, because I meant it. I was in such shock, and trying to sort out what to say to the kids; the upcoming wedding; what was going to happen to him, and on, and on, and on...

When my daughter came home from her date, I was still there on the floor talking to my mother-in-law. I seem to remember my daughter saying, "Mom, what are you doing on the floor talking"? I don't know what I said, but I did not tell her the truth.

It was the next day that answered she answered the telephone, and one of the men who was employed as a sub-contractor for my husband, thought he was speaking to me. He gave her some awful news that shook her to the core. It was completely unexpected on her part, and something I had hoped was in the past, once again reared its ugly head. She went white; and now something I had tried to keep hidden from my children was about to be exposed. It was a horrible time. My son-in-law, upon hearing the news the next day screamed at the top of his lungs. He was also devastated because he had looked at my husband as a mentor. Everything came to a halt. They both had a lot to deal with, especially my daughter; this was her father.

At this point our son still did not know what had happened. He was 14. But it was inevitable. He approached me the next day while I was at the piano and asked me what was going on. He insisted on knowing. If I remember correctly I think he either heard something at school, and, or sensed something was really wrong. I think I told him his dad had been arrested; so much is a blur. For some reason I seem to remember he was not completely surprised that something had been wrong.

Because of the news, our daughter and her fiancé decided to get married in November, rather than December. Everything had been in place for the wedding, etc. but it was just too much for her and her fiancé to deal with. And truthfully, I didn't know how I was going to deal with it either. The wedding was now only for family, and no longer at the church, but rather at the college chapel. It was certainly understandable that the two of them just wanted to "get away from it all". My father's wife and I made a beautiful hat for my daughter to wear with the wedding gown. We also made a beautiful bouquet for her, and flowers for her maid of honor. My 14-year-old son played the organ, and her grandfather, my father, walked her down the aisle. The wedding was lovely, and she was beautiful, and we all made the best of a very difficult time.

We had a small reception with both families. Then the two of them went on their honeymoon. I cannot imagine how hurt she must have been to have had all this happen a couple of months before her wedding. I just can't imagine, and after all these years, when I think about it, I feel so angry at him!

I'm not sure if my husband ever fully realized the pain he caused by giving in to his sin. I'm quite sure he deeply regretted not being at the wedding, but beyond that, I'm not sure. He now had, in addition to that, something else to worry about. An upcoming trial.

I think everyone was screaming at this time in our lives, either using our inside voice, or our outside one. It didn't matter because the Lord heard us all. This time I insisted that my husband move out; I gave him six weeks to find a place. I felt bad that I insisted that he leave. I could imagine how awful he felt at being asked to leave his home, but gone was my resolve to stick with him. And can you understand that I felt guilty about that? I felt sorry for him. I made sure he had pots and pans, and anything else that was absolutely necessary for him to have on move out day.

What about our children? If I go back in my mind to all this trauma in their lives, I hurt so, for them. I really don't even remember how we got through those days; any of us. It must have been by putting one foot in front of the other and just moving! I think I was tethered to the Lord and He was pulling me along.

SEPTEMBER 29, 1984   We are once again separated.

OCTOBER 21, 1984

Spare the Anguish
To live today: to awake and be thankful,
To arise and accomplish,
To sleep again in awareness,
I am not alone.

Lord, spare me the anguish of the unalterable –
The need for answers for tomorrow, today.
Allow me the absence of worry
For tomorrow's tomorrow
As I live today.

At this time I began having panic attacks while driving. I had to always have in my mind a plan of escape when I pulled up to a stop sign, or came to a red light. I had to roll down the window, turn on the radio, make noise, anything at all until my car was again moving. It was quite scary. I often felt like I would pass out. It didn't affect me if someone was in the car with me, but rather when I was alone. I wore my husband's shame as my own, and at certain times I could not leave the house without wearing sunglasses. Like a child playing peek-a-boo with her hands in front of her eyes, I thought people couldn't see me behind the dark glasses.

This time he and I knew there would be a trial.

OCTOBER 26, 1984   Purpose through repentance

I may have remorse and regret, and my spirit in two may rent, but true purpose has not been met until I have been willing to repent.

Repentance is not just being sorry, not just feeling regret; it involves changing.

I prayed, and I asked the Lord to please keep him out of jail. The thing of it is, he really did belong there, but I was worried what would happen to him if he was sent there.

NOVEMBER 17, 1984   I put myself in my husband's place, and penned the following poem. All this is how I imagined him to be feeling. It is good to be able to put oneself in the place of another at times, but I really think it kept me from seriously looking at reality, and prolonged the inevitable.

My Name

When I look down the long road darkness I do see:
darkness all around and deep inside of me.
No other path to follow - only one, no more.
Will this be the same - like the one I walked before?

Shadowed figures in the night
My stopped-up ears, my blinded sight.
I will not move. I'll stand here still.
But here it comes - that awful chill!

I'm cold, I'm old, I see no light –
Know no wrong, desire no right.
I feel no anger, feel no pain –

Want no answer, know not my name.

I work, I play, eat and sleep,
Talk the Word, live deceit.

Again, I turned and ran back
To the place where I had been –
Made my choice, this is the way,
And now I'm caught again.

This spot is so familiar - just like it was before.
I'll settle in, feels like me –
This is my place, worth nothing more.

Repeat my actions, play my game;
Does not matter - know not my name.

Is this torment or is this fun?
How many am I, or am I one?

I've chosen, I'm stuck, can't hear, can't see.
All that I wanted has destroyed me.

Yet, still I'm alive! Though blinded and deaf
Still there is Truth - hope is not dead yet!

Lord God, Merciful One, You've shown me the way -
Still I must choose.
Thank-you for today.
Give me the courage to give up my game.
Help me to search for and, at last, find my name.

NOVEMBER 19, 1984

Pulled

Lord, You must surely limit Your power,
You, must certainly exercise control,
For day by day –
Hour by hour,

On your heart, my desires pull.

There are times we must surely pull on the heartstrings of the Lord; He is the only one who can perfectly handle that kind of pressure. We feel we need something to change now. Now, Lord, please!

Who Can?
Who can counsel the Lord, who can guide His way?
And to induce Him to act, who enough can pay?

"'For who hath known the mind of the Lord, that he may instruct him' (New King James Version, 1 Cor. 2.16)?"

"'For who has known the mind of the Lord and who has understood his thoughts, or who has (ever) been his counselor' (Amplified, Rom. 11.34)?)

We may not always know why we do the things we do, and we surely don't always know why the Lord allows certain things to happen, nor do we know why He does what He does, but the one thing that is absolute is that He, Himself, always knows what he is doing. He is God.

23
Waiting in the Desert

NOVEMBER, 1984   Once again I'm sitting on the living room
floor, looking out the living room window.

The Tree
Outside my living room window
Stands a barren tree
Purged by the breath of God
Of all decaying leaves.

High within her branches
Swings a battered nest
Rocked by the breath of God,
The tree and her guest.

Fallen leaves in disarray
Pruned from out their space
Designed by the breath of God
For Him a working place.

Branches in community
Wait for winter's snowing
Blown by the breath of God
White covering meant for growing.

Icicles form crystal and clear
But for a season they cling,
Until the melting breath of God
Once again brings spring.

Alive as promised tiny buds
Burst forth upon each branch

Opening to the breath of God
They join Him in a dance.

Fluttering high within the nest
A bird among the leaves
As before the breath of God
Breathed life into the tree.

So it goes the same with man,
We live and die,
And then the breath of God in sweetness
Blows upon the soul again.

"'Another parable put He forth unto them, saying,
"The kingdom of heaven is like to a grain of mustard
seed which a man took, and sowed in his field:
Which indeed is the least of all seeds: but when it is
grown, it is the greatest among herbs, and becometh
a tree, so that the birds of the air come and lodge in
the branches thereof"' (King James Version, Matt.
13.31-32)."

NOVEMBER 1984   The following poem is in reference to the
marriage supper of the Lamb (Jesus) in the Bible. It can be found in
Revelation chapter 19. Much of the poem is a picture I see in my mind.

This Day We Shall Dine
I walked up to the door
And wanted to go in
Night was fast approaching
My eyesight growing dim.

I knocked with expectation,
He answered it with ease,
And then His invitation,
"Come in and join us, please."

He had others there for me to meet
As we walked across the floor,

"We'll wait for the rest before we eat",
Then again a knock at the door.

He smiled at us in a tender way
And then with His arms opened wide,
Greeted the newcomers standing there
And drew them close to His side.

"Welcome, my friends, we've been waiting for you."
Then he handed us a robe,
Each one was new.

His eyes were ablaze, shining as fire,
The robe he wore dyed deep blood red
He spoke the truth and carried a rod,
And many the crowns He wore on His head.

We all talked together before sitting down
And then as His custom, we were given a crown.
"This day we shall dine." He began to break bread
And poured out the wine to share as we fed.

The cup he passed round held the wine of His choice
And each word of the toast the wonder of His voice.
We joined Him in laughter as we gave Him our fears
And gladly relinquished all sorrow and tears.

In awe, we saw each other change
And leave all earthly ties
As He revealed eternity from the depths of His eyes.

His radiance was the Light reflected on each face
We were home at last and finished was our race.

Then a child who sat beside Him
Rose from out her seat
And lay her crown, a pearly one,
At the Savior's feet.
"Thank-you for the bread, Lord,

And for your favorite wine
But the crown upon my head, Lord,
I want it to be Thine."

Then voice opened in song
And rapturous were the sounds
As feet from every nation
Brought to Him their crowns.

We all stood 'round the throne,
The Spirit wooed each one
Promised to the Father
Paid for by the Son.

Death had been defeated,
The Bride united with the Son,
Their purpose at last completed,
We saw all three embrace as one.

The truth is we never have to knock on the door of heaven. If we know the Lord, we know that we will immediately be with him when we die. It says so in 2 Corinthians.

"'We are confident, yes, well pleased rather to be absent from the body and to be present with the Lord' (VERSION 2 Cor. 5.8)."

This is true if we each have confessed that we are sinners, and accept Jesus Christ as our Savior. If one does not believe the Bible is God's word, and will not acknowledge their need of a Savior, they will not be with Him when they die.

NOVEMBER 1984   My husband was out on bail. His trial was set for February. We continued to talk almost daily. I worried how I would ever support our children if he went to jail. (Many of you out there in reader-land have done an excellent job of doing that. I am truly sad that you have had to do so; you are faithful in a most important way.) I worried what would happen to him if he did go to jail; he would not be treated kindly, I was sure. And I prayed.

And I leaned heavily, at times, on my friends. Friends are those people in your life you can count on. They need to be able to count on you, as well. I have been so fortunate to have friends by my side my whole life. Some of you are my game-buddies; we enjoy the challenges a good game brings. Some of you are on my call list for "let's do lunch" where we catch up on all that is going on in our lives. Some of you are my Sunday-friends, those people I usually connect with when I walk in the church door; people I look forward to seeing each week, and who I miss if one of us isn't there. Some of you have been with me for many years, and contributed to my life by being encouragers, and praying friends. I would say that each one of you I could trust with my heart. This list includes two pastors, and my children. I place the utmost value on each of you. You know who you are.

DECEMBER 31, 1984

To My Friends
I thanked the Lord for you today –
For encouragement and love,
And for the grace-filled wisdom given from above.

I thanked the Lord for you today –
For hugs and smiles so warm,
or arms that reach, and greetings sweet, and hope,
again reborn.

I thanked the Lord for you today –
For counsel wisely shared,
For time and thoughts in your day to show me that
you cared.

I thanked the Lord for you today
Though you have caused great pain.
I asked the Lord to bless you with freedom, friends,
and gain.

"A friend is what the heart needs at all times"
Henry Van Dyke [5]

I was, and am so blessed to have Godly friends in my life, and Godly counselors. But they can't compare to the truth that God continued to walk with me. I'm sure at times he was weeping over the catastrophic scene he saw before Him.

It might be noted here, and well worth taking to heart, that I never wanted to be a bitter person. I had heard, and knew people who could not get past a major hurt, and lived with a bitter heart the rest of their lives. Somewhere I heard that when we have "bad" feelings toward another person, we should pray for good things for them. I have put that into practice and it is a wonderful, wonderful help at ridding my heart of harmful attitudes. It is not a quick fix, but rather a means to freedom. If you have never tried it, I hope you will; for your sake.

Jesus said it best in Matthew,

"'But I say unto you, Love your enemies, bless them that curse you, do good to them that hate you, and pray for them which despitefully use you, and persecute you' (King James Version, Matt. 5.44)."

It is true that I had moments of anger. I said things I wish I had not said. At times, I raged. One time I broke a lamp out of extreme frustration because I could do nothing at all to stop the downward road I was a partner on. There were times I hated to look in the mirror at myself because I was not all that I thought I should be; I did not like the person I was. I learned to be suspicious, and I tried hard to control my husband's behavior in order to keep everything intact. I often felt trapped. There were times I wished he would die. I did not know how to get out of the trap I was in, and it was often a very scary place. I was "walled in"; "walled in" by fear, walled-in by faith, and walled-in by an unknown future.

To the best of my recollection the Lord enabled me to be loving and supportive of my children. Somehow, when they were around I buried all my negative feelings, and I acted like everything was okay. I no longer could discern when things really were okay, and when there was true reason for alarm. I wanted our children to have security, and I wanted them to have respect for their father, because I knew the dangers they could encounter if they didn't. Even when the reality of the separations, presented itself, I still acted like things would be okay. When there is so much denial and pretending going on real protection is minimal no matter what the intent of the heart is.

I do think there were times when our children were aware of the tension and unhappiness, the pretending.

Once I remember sitting in the bedroom in the dark, in the corner, and my little girl slipped a note under the door to me. She said, "Mommy, don't be sad". My heart breaks still when I think how she must have felt, and how she was trying to fix her mommy so she could be again happy.

There was also a genuine optimistic component in all of this madness. I truly did believe that during those early separations that we could get back on track, and make it work. Following the first two separations, it was with joy and pleasure when we were once again a family. It lasted for a time. This was how I felt; I don't know if my children would tell you differently.

What have you waited for in your life? The birth of a child; an upcoming wedding; a long-awaited reunion; a first date; news from someone far away; the healing of your body, or mind, or spirit; a promotion; perhaps even an impending death of one near to you. We all have times of waiting. We have varying emotions during our waiting time, and we have various attitudes toward waiting, and we also have options. Yes, you do.

What do you do while you are waiting? Pace the floor, drown yourself in food or drink? Do you get snippy with others or impatient with yourself? Do you become discouraged, and decide just to exist during the waiting time?

There have been many times in my life when I have had to wait. Sometimes a few days, sometimes a couple of months, and sometimes years. Much of the waiting has been difficult, and I have not often waited patiently. But I have found there is little we can do to hurry things up. Because of that truth, there must be a way to wait, and not fret and fear. Without a doubt, there is the danger of falling into the pit of victims. What I try to remember to do, from a practical standpoint, is to do something constructive during the waiting period, and to reach out to others who may also be waiting. What I try to remember is that ultimately God has everything in His control, and He has a perfect time for our waiting to end.

JANUARY 1, 1985   Sustain only in Your presence

> "'The mountain shall be Thine (King James Version, Josh. 17.18)."

JANUARY 18, 1985, 3:15 A.M. I was reading Psalm chapter 46 and I found comfort in reading the words of the Lord; great comfort, but could be reduced to fear when I thought of circumstances.

> "'God is our refuge and strength, a very present help in trouble. Therefore will not we fear, though the earth be moved' (King James Version, Ps. 46.1-3)."

JANUARY 29, 1985   In my journal I found the names of those people who were on my mind this day, and how I prayed for each one, including myself. Following the prayer is the subsequent verse I prayed Each one of the following 5 verses is taken from the King James Version Bible.
My husband, that he would choose truth.

> "'Remove from me the way of lying: and grant me thy law graciously. I have chosen the way of truth: thy judgments have I laid before me' (King James Version, Ps. 119:29-30)."

Our son, the he would desire Lord more than gold; love His word.

> "'Make me to understand the way of thy precepts: so shall I talk of thy wondrous works' (King James Version, Ps. 119:27)."

> "'Incline my heart unto thy testimonies, and not to covetousness' (King James Version, Ps. 119:36)."

Our daughter, that she would walk in the way of good judgment.

"'Teach me good judgment and knowledge: for I have believed thy commandments' (King James Version, Ps. 119:66)."

And for myself, that I may I have peace and not be offended easily.

"'Great peace have they which love thy law: and nothing shall offend them' (King James Version, Ps. 119:165)."

"'For my soul trusts in thee, yes, in the shadow of thy wings will I make my refuge until these calamities be over-past' (King James Version, Ps. 57.1)."

This psalm has been a comfort to me.

FEBRUARY 17, 1985   Sunday. I was so preoccupied today I got nothing out of the message.

FEBRUARY 19, 1985

Pressure
I feel pressure.
I feel pressure.
I feel pressure.

FEBRUARY 19, 1985   The days keep right on passing by. I feel the pressure of the up-coming trial. I feel increasing pressure of where to move, when to move, a job? I never minded moving when my husband was with me, however this time he won't be.

FEBRUARY 21, 1985   I was so upset today; I spent the whole day with a friend. It was helpful to realize again that the Lord is in control. I am frightened at night, but the Lord has helping power. I want Him to have the victory.

When the trial came, I went, as did my father-in-law. It was so hard.

My husband wasn't convicted. He was free, but not really. There was a tremendous amount of devastation in our family. That was the end of family life as we knew it.

But God was merciful. I don't know why, but He was. He sees a bigger picture than we do.

MARCH 4, 1985

"'But He, being full of compassion, forgave their iniquity, and destroyed them not: yes, many a time turned he his anger away, and did not stir up all his wrath' (King James Version, Ps. 78:35)."

APRIL 16, 1985   For weeks in my mind I keep hearing,

"'You shall not need to fight in this battle; set yourselves, stand ye still, and see the salvation of the Lord" (King James Version, 2 Chron. 20.17)."

MAY 7, 1985   I feel so needy at this time. Lord, please give me some meaning to my life. I need to laugh. I need to know I have great value; I need wholeness, Lord.

I Need

Lord, please, give me some meaning to my life.
I need to laugh.
I need to know I have value.
I need wholeness, Lord.
I need Your security.

MAY 23, 1985   This particular day I was thinking of the Lord, and wondering what He looks like. Have you ever wanted so much to see Him? I think this poem shows the desire of anyone who is so curious about the one Who loves her; desiring to know what He looks like, what He sounds like, and what it would be like to touch Him. Jesus walked here on earth, but those of us alive today did not have the opportunity to experience Him in the flesh. But would we have appreciated Him? I really hope so. Many saw Him repeatedly, and still didn't.

"'Then I saw heaven opened and behold a white horse; and he that sat upon him was called "Faithful and True, and in righteousness he doth judge and make war. His eyes were as a flame of fire, and on his head were many crowns; and he had a name written that no man knew but he himself' (King James Version, Rev. 19:11-12a).'"

What Color Are Your Eyes, Lord?
What color are your eyes, Lord,
Brown, blue, or green?
How tall do you stand,
And when will you be seen?

What color are your eyes, Lord,
Green, brown, or blue?
What about your heritage –
Are you still a Jew?

What color are your eyes, Lord,
Blue, green, or brown?
When you speak in heaven, tell me,
How does your voice sound?

And what about your hands,
Could I tell them apart?
Would their size be very large –
The same way as Your heart?

Will your eyes have a color
When I look into your face?
Do your hands have a size?
Does your height reveal your grace?

Is your skin somewhat darker?
Would I think you a handsome Jew?
Will you walk each day among us
And let us question You?

And what about the colors
You chose for here below –
Do you have a favorite one?
I would like to know.

Do you often cry real tears, Lord?
Please save some for me to see.
Do You still have your scars?
And do you look like 33?

May I be swept up in Your laughter
And one day shed my fear.
I think Your eyes go on forever...
And we'll one day share the years.

MAY 25, 1985

What's Done Is Done Is Done
If you tell me I must sing,
I'll ask you to write me a song.
If you tell me to "take a hike",
I'll ask you to come along.

If you tell me not to cry,
I'll wait while you shed your tears.
If you ask me not to die,
I'll share with you my years.

If you tell me how you're hurt,
I'll help you bear the pain.
If you tell me you are poor,
I'll give to you my gain.

If you tell me life is bad,
I'll show to you the good.
If you say that you are hungry,
I'll share with you my food.

If you say you want to leave me,

I'll pack so you can go.
If you say you'll never grieve me,
I'll reap what you will sow.

If you say your spirit's aching,
I'll help you learn to mend.
If you say your heart is breaking,
I'll say "then build again."

If you say that it is over,
And all is in the past,
I'll tell you this is "now",
and tomorrow's in your grasp.

If you ask me to forgive you,
I'll say, "I need forgiveness, too."
What's done, is done, is done –
And that we can't undo.

MAY 25, 1985

Beckon
Love calls me to look up into the highest Heaven
And reach for the highest star.
It wraps me up in warmth and gives me life.

My heart peels off the layers of my darkened soul,
And I am drenched in Light.

Oh, God! I want to come out of this prison of fear.
Help me to find the key, and to set myself free.

Yes, I lived inside myself, often; others didn't realize it. On the outside I seemed like I had everything in control; on the inside I was always afraid. But I had worn a mask for so, so long that it became natural. It helped me cope with my fear; at least I thought it did.

JUNE 15, 1985

The Hope Giver
Strength, kind, purest of mind, weeps, reaps, grows;
Patiently sows, feels, heals, bares, wonderfully cares;
Bends, mends, life, knife, pain, gain, teacher;
Preacher, soul, whole, love.
Faithful.

"'Let us hold fast the confession of our hope without wavering, for He who promised is faithful' (King James Version, Heb. 10:23)."

24
The Decision Forthcoming

I was in turmoil for at least a year about whether I should get a divorce, or not; and without a doubt I called on the Lord for discernment. I didn't want to do the wrong thing in God's eyes. One does not want to take God's plan lightly, and His plan was for a marriage to last forever. I was afraid if my husband ever did change, God would say to me, "I told you so". God is not like that, but still I was afraid of making a wrong decision. My initial decision already brought my children and me so much pain. I struggled month after month as I talked to the psychologist, and a friend. I'm quite sure they got very tired of my wrestling, but they exhibited great patience with me.

I finally made my decision to file for divorce. I never doubted my decision once it was made. It was, however, an extremely difficult and painful decision to make.

My husband fought the divorce tooth and nail, and sent me letters frequently about how he had changed, but trust was completely broken at this point, and I was now scared to death to believe what I had heard so often. I could not discern what was the truth, and what wasn't. A mate should never have to be in the place of having to discern that kind of thing. Truth and Trust are the foundation of marriage. He would not sign the papers, and so it took three years for the divorce to be finalized.

I will not say our lives were ruined, but they could have been. The marriage, however, was completely broken. I have no doubt until the day he died, he regretted the choices he made. There were many people who were hurt by my husband's choices: Our parents, our children, our friends, our church family, and others, some of whom we will never realize.

I am still amazed when I think of all our family went through, and not only survived, but grew to once again love one another. That is only because God was merciful. I don't know why. He didn't have to be, and He still would have been God. I hope it was for the children.

AUGUST 7,1985, 5:30 A.M.

The Artist and the Poet

Picture a diamond on a chain
Before the eyes of a girl.
Think of the diver with oyster in hand,
Searching for a pearl.

See how the gambler, when placing his bet,
Blows his breath on the dice.
Imagine the dreams in the heart of a man –
Each one having a price.

Look at the stars in the Heaven of lights –
One will outshine the rest.
Three coins in a fountain - three wishes afloat –
One will stand the test.

The hands of the artist paint what he sees –
What his voice cannot convey.
Yet friend poet knows well, and both would agree,
He'll find the words to say.

The diamond still sparkles, the pearl's in the deep,
The gambler has lost, the dreamers still seek.
The star shines the brighter, the wish is delayed,
The girl has grown older, the coins have decayed.

What of the artist, and poet, his friend –
The pictures they painted was that the end?
When happened to them?

Still painting the canvas, he's taking his time,
While the heart of the poet gives life to a rhyme.

One's giving color, one's adding words.

Blended are rain and sun.
A promise is made, a rainbow appears –
Artist and poet and painting are one.

AUGUST 8, 1985

A Promise - A Pain
What is as new as a baby born –
The very first minute of life?
What is as old as a heart that is torn
By death, hopelessness, strife?

Dear little baby, wise beyond years,
Water your soul with fresh baby tears.
Dear weatherworn heart, look to the snow,
As it melts with sun - new life soon to grow.

You each hold a promise,
You each share a pain.
One needs the other
To give each the gain.

AUGUST 8, 1985

Holy Spirit
O Holy Spirit,
Search me,
Reveal me,
Set me free.

One morning I woke up and heard the birds outside my
bedroom window. Without warning tears began to trickle down my
face. My sadness overwhelmed me. I was lonely, I missed my husband.
I missed the future I had so hoped for. I was not wavering in my
decision, but it was still painful.

AUGUST 9, 1985, 5:30 A.M.

Tears
I woke up this morning as it was growing light –
The birds began to chirp as they prepared for flight.
I opened up my eyes and the tears began to roll
And I wanted someone next to my soul.

The tears, they just keep coming,
As if they're in a race.
The opened door of my inner room
Is running down my face.

"'Rivers of water run down from my eyes, because
men do not keep Your law' (New King James Version,
Ps. 119:136)."

Without a doubt, my husband was hurting too. So was God.
He never wanted any of this to happen. I believe He cried with us. This
was not good for us, and this was not good for His glory. But He was
undaunted.

SEPTEMBER 1985

Help Me
Help me be, Lord, who I am.
Take from me the words
That hide my heart and feed the sham.

When you look into my eyes, Lord,
What do you see in the storehouse of my soul?

We become deceptive, covering truth with words.

Searching
No place for me to lean,
So in between I wander.
Searching for a tree that is not withered, or cut
down.

And in between a lovely poem which shows how pain can produce bitterness, or, the thorns can bring forth understanding, and compassion for those who are hurting.

SEPTEMBER 25, 1985, 12:00 A.M.

Midnight Rose
A beautiful rose he gave me,
Special I could tell,
From his heavenly garden
And everlasting well.

I fashioned me a basket
Of strong and natural reed
And placed the rose and its thorn
There beside my need.

The fragrance slowly drifted
From within to within
The color and the odor
Painted and perfumed by Him.

Soon he gave another
And then he gave some more
Filling up my basket
Fuller than before.

Each rose comes with a message
And tender is its name
The shades are very different
Their fragrance is the same.

Yellow reflects the seasons of life;
The message of pink is hope.
White bathes me in accepting love,
As red unwinds the rope.

Their fragrance surrounds me then onward it moves
searching and calling as others it woos.

The thorns prick my spirit and cause me to bleed
So I fix my eyes on the colors as the thorns complete
their deed.

My wounds begin healing
Washing out fear
And soon in my basket
More roses appear.

This basket holds a lot of wealth
And I give thanks anew
For each rose and fragrant message
Smells amazingly like you.

What do I do with these roses
And basket in my care?
Why I'll add to them my color
And then my fragrance share.

I'll give to Him the basket
A bouquet of me and thee
He'll water and prune and deliver
And hand us out for free.

To people who are waiting
With spirits that grieve
Standing in their place in time
Dying as they weave.

The Gardener sees,
The Gardener knows,
With love,
Each can become a rose.

SEPTEMBER 29, 1985

It Was I
Created from dust alive by a seed

Born through two people I filled a need.
I never knew you for you lived before
Now that we're gone the rest will be poor.

A hundred years from now,
No one will know my name
They'll never even realize
I've been here just the same.

A pebble on the beach, a star sent from the sky
A particle of dust, but we know it was "I."
Paths they are skipping down I skipped long ago
friends that I have known they'll never even know.

The thinking now belongs to them
And I am lost in time
My poems have vanished,
Still they were mine.

They feel the feelings with me
In the ground
I have gone from seed to dust
And never made a sound.

"'Like a dream he flies away, no more to be found,
banished like a vision of the night. The eye that saw
him will not see him again; his place will look on him
no more' (New International Version, Job 20:8-9)."

"'To everything there is a season, a time to every
purpose under the heaven. A time to be born... a
time to die' (New King James Version, Eccl. 3.1-2a)."

"'What is your life? It is a vapor, that appears for a
little time, and then vanishes away' (New King James
Version, Jas. 4.14)."

"'My substance was not hid from thee when I was
made in secret' (King James Version, PS. 139:15)."

OCTOBER 1, 1985   I wrote a sadly sweet poem about myself as a child, though much of my childhood was very enjoyable. I played all the games little kids played in the 1940s such as tag, hopscotch, and hide and seek. I climbed trees, rode a bike, roller skated, played paper dolls, colored, and played house. The one thing I do believe I felt, was lonely. Not lonely because I had no friends, because I did, but lonely because there was a part of me that wasn't quite reached. It is a difficult thing to put into words, but if you have felt it, you will understand what I'm trying to say.

I would like to encourage you to look at the little child you were, and love that little girl or boy. Every child deserves love, and you do to.

Melancholy Tunes
If I could play as I once did
This is what I'd do:
I'd climb the trees, hang by my knees,
Play a game of hop-scotch, too.

Or I would sit and think,
Get lost inside my mind,
Or go up to the attic
Where treasures I could find.

I liked to be within my room
And organize my things
Or outside on the playground
Where high I'd go on swings.

I'd often practice motherhood,
Sometimes a nurse I'd be.
I even played "librarian" –
So many parts of me.

I loved to color with new crayons,
The start of school in fall,
Pencils in cases, and colored erasers,
The smell of waiting halls.

Lots of books I'd read –
This I loved to do.
I'd jump inside the pages
With the Bobbsey Twins and Nancy Drew.

Scrapbook of the movie stars,
Paper dolls with fancy clothes,
Cowboys and Indians, or musicals
Were my very favorite picture shows.

Even as a child, when melancholy tunes would start,
we'd be as one, and then, when done,
The music and message would know my heart.

OCTOBER 1, 1985

My Mirror
If you look into my mirror,
I know what you might see
A very little girl
Inside this woman - me.

I close my eyes and can feel her
And how I wish I knew
If this little girl
Would be this woman, too.

My life is in the pages
Of all the books she read
It's hanging from the maple tree
And playhouse in the shed.

I'm with her in the attic
Alone as we can be
Or sitting on the front porch
Sharing dreams she sees.

Is she whom I'm protecting
Behind my grown-up years?

The mirror looks beyond the shades
That guard her childish fears.

I've got to hide her, got to run
And shield her from the lies
Go up to the attic and meet her there
And cover up her eyes.

That place is in the past now,
The years got in the way
But the child is alive and how I cried
To be like her today.

And so my path goes back and forth
And no one ever knows
Except the mirror and the eyes
That watch her as she grows.

OCTOBER 10, 1985

Unseen
I only thought I saw, but what I saw was not the
thing I should have seen, the thing I should have got!

There is "blind",
And there is "blind",
And they can be
Two of a different kind.

OCTOBER 15, 1985　　It was during this time I began reading
books written by Leo Buscaglia, who was dubbed the "Love Doctor".
He was nicknamed this because after he would speak to an audience
he would invite them to come up on stage for a hug. I believe he was a
very good man who desired to reach out to people and help them feel
loved. As to his spiritual condition, I don't know.

OCTOBER 21, 1985

Buscaglia
While driving down the road today
And looking at the trees
I thought of you, Buscaglia,
And how you love the leaves.

The colors are magnificent
At this time of year
Buscaglia you'd go crazy
If you were living here.

There's red and orange, yellow and green,
Salmon pink, and brown
Pieces of the rainbow
Falling to the ground.

The scent that floats down with them
Is of a faithful kind
Past and present and future
Impressions on the mind.

Buscaglia, I hope you're planning
A visit from your home in Southern "C."
Hurry up, please don't miss
The changing of the leaves.

One more thing, Buscaglia,
I love the way you write
The way you feel makes me squeal
With pure and sweet delight.

Lover of the Leaves
Remember in the days of old
When the Lord God changed a name
From one thing to another
And the person no longer the same?

I'm changing yours, Buscaglia,
To "Lover of the Leaves" –

The great Italian Lover
and friend to all the trees.

Traveling With Buscaglia

I'd love to travel with Buscaglia
To all the places he has seen
Walk the roads of Saigon
And see the gorge in Bali green.

I find a certain fascination
In his reaching out to live
He wraps his arms around
All others want to give.

Language is a barrier small,
"Class" is soon erased
In each reception, no deception
They share a warm embrace.

Sweet man, you do intrigue me
And I would wish for you
That as you're loving others,
Someone will love you, too.

I sent these poems to Dr. Leo Buscaglia, and he responded with a note thanking me. I still have that note. I thought it was very kind of him to respond.

I do not necessarily know what was on my mind when I wrote this next poem. I do know that these people all were in the presence of Jesus during His earthly life. He ministered to each of them with mercy and care.

October 26, 1985

Had I Been the Bride

Had I been in the garden a flower, when you cried
I would have bloomed the whole night through
Had I been by your side.

Had I been a sister when Martha cooked the meat
I could have joined with Mary
And listened at your feet.

And when you called the children the line I might
have led
To once again come closer –
Feel your hands upon my head.

Had I been on the boat when you walked upon the
sea,
I would have jumped with Peter
If you had called to me.

And when around the table, John leaned upon your
breast
Wish I had been there with you
To enjoy that place of rest.

I see a woman bending down in quiet desperation
Touch the hem of your dusty robe
In hopeful expectation.

You turned and called the touch, there came a
trembling soul,
"Be of good comfort, go in peace,
Your faith has made you whole."

Remember the day the family came
The disciples asked which had sinned
The parents, the son, or all of them,
Because of the blindness of him.

"The Light of the world, I am" You said,
Then you spat upon the ground,
Anointed his eyes, sent him away to wash,
Then his sight he found.
Could I have been a thing you used,
I would have chosen three –

The cup you held, the robe you wore,
The sand beneath your knee.

One you shared with others,
One kept you warm,
One you used on bended knee, writing on its form.

Like the day they brought her to you
And wanted to have her stoned
You stooped to the ground and wrote in the sand
Desiring they leave her alone.

On they continued with questions and more,
You arose with one of your own:
"Is anyone here that has never sinned?
You may cast the first stone."

You stooped down again, continued to write,
Slowly they each walked away
Again, you arose to find them all gone,
To her, you had words to say.

"Has no man condemned thee? Neither do I;
Go woman sin no more."
How lucky she was to stand there with you,
Protected, freed, and adored.

And in Cana, at the wedding had I been the bride
I would have searched the whole crowd through
To ask you to my side.

I would have toasted one with you,
The rich and perfect wine
We'd be a three-fold cord,
Unbroken, intertwined.

"'A three-fold cord is not quickly broken' (New King
James Version, Eccles. 4.12b)."

I've always loved the above verse. It has such unity and strength in it. That is the way a marriage is supposed to be. That is the way our relationship with the Lord is to be. Strong, permanent, and unified. This is a verse my son and daughter-in-law used in their wedding.

NOVEMBER 8, 1985, 6:20 A.M.

"'Bring my soul out of prison (the desert) that I may praise Thy name' (King James Version, Ps. 142:7)."

The Key
Person of pretense, Person of fear,
Person of sorrow Sitting here.
Behind locked doors in your room
Dying slowly In the womb.

Someone is coming someone is here
He has the keys To help you my dear.

The key to my heart is Truth,
For it unlocks the door of suspicion,
And inside is my child, and my Trust.

The key to my heart is Time,
For patience unlocks the door of urgency,
And inside is my child and my Hope.

The key to my heart is Temperance,
For it unlocks the door of selfishness,
And inside is my child and my affection.

The key to my heart is Touch,
For it unlocks the door of fear,
And inside is my child and my Warmth.

The key to my heart is Tenderness,
For it unlocks the door of self-protection,
And inside is my child and my Heart.

The key to my heart is Transparency,
For it unlocks the door of darkness,
And inside is my child and my Essence.

When all the doors are opened,
And all the rooms are bare;
Seen with the center, Love is standing there;

Reaching out to others,
Holding out the keys,
Multiplied from heart
The gifts given to me.

NOVEMBER 12, 1985 6:00 P.M.

Fire
See the coals Lying untouched
Cold, waiting to be stoked.
See the match, on the hearth,
Power, in one designed stroke;

See the hand Reaching out,
Master of the fire;
Hear the crackle Singing out,
Born A blazing choir.

Rising flames Create an illusion,
Companion In the night.
Only a shadow, Delicious delusion
Appearing In fire light.

See within the backdrop,
Perfect haven Remaining, Colorful fingers.
And the heart Is warmed,
As the inventive Imagination lingers.

Slowly the fire ebbs and on the coal's fading embers
Lies the heart as memory remembers.

25
Soul Desert

I continued to write. I continued to ask questions of God. I was still waiting for my husband to sign the divorce papers. And I still felt like I was in a desert. But keep in mind that God is concerned with what happens in a desert, and sometimes new life begins because of the process of walking there.

DECEMBER 4, 1986, 2:45 A.M I am 45 years old   This poem I wrote the following year in December, but seems appropriate to put here.

Desert Place
I've been wandering in the desert, Lord,
For over 30 years –
Walking around in circles,
Parading with my fears.

You promised You would lead me
And ever be my Guide.
Yet, even as I search,
Your hand You seem to hide.

You give me shelter, food and drink –
I try not to complain –
But the time is growing short
And my searching seems in vain.

Not a bit of this makes sense:
The scales upon my eyes,
The deafness of my ears,
The ceiling to my cries.

I feel just like a peddler
With burdens in a sack:
Useless virtues all tied up
And carried on my back.

The days keep moving on
And in this death I'm caught.
This all seems such a waste, Lord,
If my freedom You have bought.

The wandering makes me dry
And I am oft in doubt.
Is this to be my grave,
Or will You lead my out?

I hear the words You have said –
Verse by verse I'm bound
By the knowings in my head,
Yet still I drag around.

Your Book I search to no avail –
One of us is lost.
My heart and life are still in jail
Though You have paid the cost.

I'm tired of all the trudging
Through deep and lonely sand:
Eating desert manna
And searching for your plan.

This trek is such a drain.
The dryness of this place
Makes my freedom seem illusive –
Like the presence of Your face.

Are You going to leave me wandering
In the deepness of my sighs,
Or will You set my spirit free
And open up my eyes.

"'Sing to God, sing praises to His name; cast up a highway for Him who rides through the deserts; His name is the Lord, be in high spirits and glory before Him' (Amplified, Ps. 68:4)!"

NOVEMBER 23, 1985, 11:15 P.M.

The Race
I feel as though I'm in a race
Running down the track
Facing hurdles one by one
Tired of looking back.

The barriers stand before me
Many a different size,
And I'm jumping over each
To where the victory lies.

And when I conquer on
I slow and rest awhile
And then it's time to rise again
And run another mile.

The race I run is all my own
Except for he who guides me
The face I wear I know alone
Though others run beside me.

Sometimes I stumble, even fall,
Often drag, and at times, crawl.
Then up again at steady pace,
"Hurray"! I'm back again in the race.

What is my goal? The finish line,
Collect the prize I've won,
With His voice, I want to hear
His words to me, "Well done!"

What will I have to give him

When I look into His face
My hands, my heart, for from the start,
Along beside,
He was my Guide, my voice, my song,
For all along,
He ran with me the race.

The prize for me at this time was to hear Him say, "Well done". I think to hear Him say that would make it all worth running the race.

Therefore since we are surrounded by such a great cloud of witnesses, let us throw off everything that hinders and the sin that so easily entangles, and let us run with perseverance the race marked out for us' (New International Version, Heb. 12:1)."

In December of this year, I decided to make my own Christmas cards. For the verse inside I composed two poems which spoke of the Savior, because that is the real reason for Christmas. DECEMBER 13, 1985

"'And thou shalt call his name Jesus: for He shall save his people from their sins' (King James Version, Matt. 1.21b)."

God's Gift
God's gift to mankind
Came wrapped in love
On the wings of the wind
In the form of a dove.

His gift made an entrance
As a baby that night
Into the darkness
He came as the Light.

His gift has a purpose
Here born the plan

The way of Salvation
For the life of each man.

DECEMBER 13, 1985

"'All the earth shall worship Thee, and shall sing unto
Thee; the shall sing to Thy name. Selah' (King James
Version, Ps. 66:4)."

The Announcement
From out of the sky
Came a glorious song
Announcing the news of His birth.

From the depths of God's heart
Came Eternal Love
Salvation for man on earth.

DECEMBER 24, 1985   This particular night I was sitting in the
living room, on the floor, with my notebook, and a cup of hot
chocolate. It was Christmas eve. I was alone, as my daughter was
married, and my son was asleep in bed for the night. I began to think
of all the people who were struggling and sad on this night. So often
we forget about them, in the hustle and bustle of the holiday. I am
process now of creating a musical drama from this poem.

The Other Side of Christmas
Tomorrow is Christmas –
This, the night before.
I sit here in the quiet
And a poem knocks at my door.

I drink myself some warmth
And the words begin to weave
As somewhere in the silence,
I hear the sounds of Christmas eve.

People scurrying in the night –
Buying more bills to pay.

Mommy and Daddy had a fight –
Tomorrow's Christmas day.

Little children who cannot sleep
Wonder if they've been good enough
To get a present from Santa Claus –
A toy and clothing stuff.

See them crying silent tears
In a nursing home:
Useless and forgotten,
And missing children grown.

"Come and sit with me", they say,
"Hold my hand and care."
But only comes a sleepless night
To join a far-off stare.

The captive waits for a letter from home,
The cold hopes for a ring,
The hitchhiker thumbs on the road alone
And feels the failure sting.

Someone is screaming on Christmas eve,
Someone is laying in stench,
Someone is shooting dope up his sleeve,
Someone is kneeling by a cold park bench.

Someone is drinking too much this eve
And making himself a clown,
Trying the loneliness to relieve
By gulping the fire water down.

Someone will close his eyes in death
With no one to sit by his side;
Someone will watch her lover's last breath
And wish that he hadn't died.

Someone is walking alone in the rain,

Someone has lost a friend;
He closes his eyes to this time of pain
And waits for the sorrow to end.

Someone is stealing on Christmas eve,
Someone is beating his wife;
Someone is hanging his head in despair
And thinking of taking his life.

A tear slides down a weathered cheek –
Excitement has died for my son.
My father grew older one day this week
And a new year already is done.

Someone is giving a reason to yell,
Someone is shaking the bars of his cell,
Someone is entering the gates of hell,
While somewhere a deacon rings the old church bell.

This all seems so familiar –
I seem to understand –
For within my heart
I hear the sounds of fellow man.

Once I believed in Santa Claus,
When I was very small,
And no one ever told me,
For no one ever saw

That tonight I would be weaving,
On the eve of Christmas day,
Lives of people in a poem
That soon will pass away.

Someone's heart is growing old
Deep within a mine;
All that glitters is not gold,
And some gold doesn't shine.

JANUARY 1, 1986, 2:00 A.M.

Enough
There are not enough days in one's life
Nor pages in a book
Not enough answers to the questions "Why?",
And too much sorrow to continue to look.

There is not enough pain to feel the ache,
Too few days to die,
An abundance of nights lying awake
And too few tears to cry.

There are not enough words to tell it well,
Too few feelings to express
Icicles form and slowly adorn
The longing heart within the breast.

O Holy Fire with glowing warmth
Melt in me the frozen flame of love,
Ever alive and burning.

Yesterday's life is gone,
Tomorrow's breath is not here
Today is the moment to begin the New Year

JANUARY 5, 1986   This next poem I submitted for publication. I was given a cash prize of $25.00. The publication was put out by "The People's Voice", in Red Lion, Pennsylvania.

The real treasure of a person lies not in outward appearance, but rather behind the eyes, and in the heart and soul. It is for this, Jesus considered worth of dying for.

The Treasure
If I were to search for a treasure,
Where is the first place I'd look
Behind a wall, under a rock,
Or in the pages of a book?

n help people
d new life in Ch

are your faith, your life can be a testimor
including people like Meg.* Meg was hur
the funeral, she turned to the internet f
und our internet evangelism site, Peace
and then enrolled in one of our online
us that she prayed to receive Jesus Christ as
ul for your heart to see Meg—and many
living hope" (1 Peter 1:3, ESV).

You look at me
and see my flaws;
I look at you
and see flaws, too.
Those who love
know love deserves
a second glance;
each failure serves
another chance.
Love looks to see,
beyond the scars
and flaws, the cause;
and scars become
an honorable badge
of battles fought
and won—(or lost)
but fought!
The product, not the cost,
is what love sought.

* * *

God help us see beyond the now
to the before, and note with
tenderness what lies between—
and love the more! ■

Would I go to a museum
And walk among the halls,
Scan the artist's paintings
As they hung upon the walls?

I could dig within the earth
In hopes of finding gold,
Or sit among philosophers
And probe great minds of old.

If I searched the whole world over,
Took a journey through the skies
I'd only find the treasure sought
Behind a pair of eyes.

JANUARY 10, 1986, 6:00 P.M.

The Life of a Candle
Candle that gives light in the night.
One is enough alone to dispel darkness.
Fragrance and color united with the fire.
Wax flowing down yielding completing its purpose.

The candle slowly ebbs away,
The fire burns on with consistence,
The fragrance has left in the air
Its gentle mark of persistence.

The colorful wax in small drops on the floor
Is waiting to be molded to a candle once more.

Have you ever noticed how one candle can make a difference in a dark room? One person can make a difference too, in a very dark world.

Jesus is The Light of the World. Without Him you walk in darkness no matter how bright your path.

MARCH 27, 1986   I actually had a dream last night in which all
of this took place in the poem before. I don't know, maybe I am
represented by the different women.

A Dream, Two Jews, and The Other
Last night I had this dream in which I met two Jews
The younger one wanted to become a Rabbi
The older one present was her aged mother,
And I, myself, the third, made up the other.

Three chairs around a small corner table,
First I sat there alone.
Then the two of them came and joined me,
And the younger spoke to the grown.

Not being part of her animated conversation
I still listened to all I could see
Sitting there in number three station
I silently became one of the three.

Before they came I had been reading
And the marker on the book said, "Jew."
Slowly I raised it, hoped they would see,
Sitting there with them, I was too,

When the young one asked a question of me:
"Are you a believer in the only one God?"
Unsure how to answer my head gave a nod.

"I am a Christian, I know of whom you speak
I know what you search for, and who you seek."

Then I drew back and arose from the table,
Excused myself from what once was three
Left the cafe, went into the night,
Walked a cobbled path, alone with just me.

Outside the cafe' I looked in the windows
Saw a yellow glow, and heard glasses tinkling.

139

I stumbled and stooped for a moment,
And then the young girl was beside me
ust like a friend.

First there was one, that one was me
Then when they joined me, we became three.
I left the table, the two of them there,
I was alone, and they were a pair.

Then two became one, and one became two
No longer the circle of three.
The mother was gone, and I once alone
Found the girl walking with me.

I still think of the one with black flying hair,
Electric ideas from out eyes a glistening.
The ridiculous idea she wanted to share, a
And the mother who sat quietly listening.

Asenath Biarzani was Kurdish, and the first Jewish woman to become a rabbi. The first woman to become an ordained Jewish Rabbi was Regina Jonas, in Germany, in 1935.

MARCH 29, 1986

The Encourager
No words of thanks could ever express
The part in my life you play;
The distance I'll go would be much less,
And lonelier I'd be as I walk this way.

My heart will try to grasp the pain
So my eyes again may see
The Light, The Truth along my way,
If as you wound, you walk with me.

APRIL 18, 1986

Gentle Hands
Gentle hands upon my face
Opening up my eyes
Beckoning me to look beyond
The wall of darkened skies.

Tender hands holding mine,
Warming icy fear,
Life in human fingertips
Another presence near.

Steady feet follow mine
As I walk through the past,
Leading where mine fear to go,
To bring me peace at last.

Ears ready tuned to hearing,
The searching of my voice
Listening, ever listening
As I examine choice.

Strength for when I'm weak,
Guidance when I'm wrong,
Wisdom when I see,
Loving me to strong.

The poems above were also tributes to my counselor on whom I leaned so heavily.

JUNE 1986   In my journal, I wrote, "Longing, searching for a purpose."

Experiences
I heard about a mother who gave her baby's heart
To another child who lay a-dyin'
I heard about a boy who gave one of his eyes
To a brother blind who sat a-cryin'.

I heard about a dad who offered up the truth

To a wayward son who stood a-lyin'
I heard about a man who gave away some time
To a one in need who sat a-sighin'.

I saw a busy grandpa scoop from out a crib
A little infant child who lay a-wailin'
And read about a nurse who when she saw great
need
Gave all herself to aid the tired and ailin'.

I learned about a teacher who spent all day at school
Then some more and some, to help the failin'
And saw the strength in voice calm everyone around
The one who was a threat, and a-railin'.

I heard about a woman reaching house bound folks
By spending every day a-phonin'
And I know a man who gives away his ears
To those who sit all day with voice a-droanin'.

Still that is not enough so he gives away his arms
To people who are said and a-moanin'
And about our God who gave away his Son
To people who are lost and a-groanin'.

I talked to a mother who sat and rocked all day
A sick and frightened child with breath a-heavin'.
And also to a man whose beloved son was cryin' and
a-packin' and a-leavin'.

I read about a shepherd boy who searched for one
lost sheep though he was tired,
Cause he was a-grievin'.

And then there was the Father's Son
Who gave away his Life
To those who would believe and came receivin'

JUNE 11, 1986, 10:30 A.M.   This next poem expresses some frustration over the fact that He doesn't allow us to see His face. He has His reasons, I know. One day we will see Him face to face.

Reasons Yet Unknown

I want to see your face, Lord,
I'm really sure I do.
When I come to meet you,
I want to look at you.

I want to hear your voice,
I listen for your sound.
I tire of reading words
By which my voice I drowned.

I want to see your being
And watch the way you are
What kind of friend are you to me
To keep yourself so far?

If you can see us all at once
And you can each one know,
If you can hear before we call,
Why won't you walk below?

Why won't you take the time
To come and sit with me,
If years are like a day,
And now eternity?

You are the God with whom I speak
And I can't understand
Why you hide yourself in faith
While others hold my hand.

You know the sound of every voice
Our size without seeing,
The form and look of every face
That you brought into being.

You never have to wonder
Or play a guessing game,
You always know where we are,
Where we're going, and whence we came.

I find it most annoying
To ever be on hold.
When will you call us from on high
To join you as we're told?

For reasons yet unknown to me
In which you have delight
I'm asked to see with eyes of faith
And not my eyes of sight.

Your voice remains a mystery
And I in silence bound
I'm asked to hear with ears of faith
And not my ears of sound.

No matter how I wish,
Or what I'd think to do,
My way is still my own,
And can't determine you.

"'For now we see through a glass darkly; but then
face to face: now I know in part; but then shall I
know even as also I am known' (King James Version,
1 Cor. 13.12)."

I was still waiting for my husband to sign the divorce papers. I
never allowed him to think there was another chance for our
marriage. I also broke off all communication with his family. It was not
that I didn't love them but I didn't want them to feel in the middle,
and I believe that is what would have happened. I did not want any of
them trying to convince me to return to him either. I felt I couldn't be
part of them and not feel pressured to also be part of him. In looking
back one thing I would have done differently is to communicate with
them my reason for pulling away.

JUNE 11, 1986   I remember the physical feelings clearly when I wrote "Trapped", because my entire insides felt shaky, like all my nerves were outside my skin. And you can sense the depression?

Death looks for a partner to enslave half of the heart divided by fear.

Include me, O Lord, in the cause of the brave for what virtue is there in living here?

Trapped

I feel at times deep within
Electric current moving
Though trapped by layers and layers of skin
Awaiting a signal long overdue.

Each part is woven in purposeful care
Yet barren with absence of aim
Enclosed and imprisoned in bars of despair
And pointlessly trying to tame.

Frenzied veins and vessels
That shout in harmony with kindred soul,
Postponing a hoped-for fruitful breakout
'Til the time of awareness of goal.

Explosion will rend the bars that bind,
Fragments will fly through the air
A harvest together of heart and mind
Engages potential in waiting there.

Death looks for a partner
To enslave half of the heart divided by fear.
Include me, O Lord, in the cause of the brave
For what virtue is there in living here?

AUGUST 19, 1986   I'm all tied up and tight inside.

Beyond

I wish I could get beyond

The trapping of my mind,
Discover what it is
That still I need to find.

Live before the essential beat
That set my life apart
Know me then before began
The wrapping of my heart.

Twice I've lived these years
Still the binding lasts
And as I eat the present
I'm rifting up the past.

All around unraveled
Scattered on the floor
Are the ribbons of my life
That brought me to your door.

Though I've searched the accumulation
Before us on the ground
I sense within the feeling still
A ribbon has me bound.

For all the throwing up
In trying to get free
This ribbon like a cord
Has got its hold on me.

It's coming from my navel
Many years in length
And wraps around my person
As it gathers strength.

It sometimes chokes expression
And tries to blind my eyes
Yet a strong impression says
My heart believes a lie.
As at times a fleeting glance

Just outside my sight
Sees the cord is an illusion
That keeps me bound in fright.

What is this fear I feel of life
And in each face I see;
That often stifles who I am
And seeks to conquer me.

AUGUST 19-20, 1986

My Savior's Touch

If I saw Him but once,
Would the sight of Him remain?
Could I be satisfied
If I saw Him not again?

If I heard Him but once,
Would His voice stay in my ears?
Could His sound in me alive
Be heard throughout the years?

If I touched Him but once,
And my heart in fullness came,
Would His touch be ever with me,
Could my life be 'ere the same?

When the veil receives the light,
The sight of Him will be
The most exciting sight
These eyes of mine will see.

His touch will make me whole,
Heal the scars upon my soul,
In a crowd a million size,
His voice I'll recognize.

Without a trace of blindness dim,
Face to face I will see Him.

Silent ears, no longer bound,
His voice released, I'll know His sound.
Imagination discarded crutch,
One day I'll know my Savior's touch.

O, that day! What a day that will be!!!

"'That which was from the beginning, which we have
heard, which we have seen with our eyes, which we
have looked upon, and our hands have handled,
concerning the Word (Jesus) of Life' (New King
James Version, 1 John 1.1)."

OCTOBER 13, 1986   This was a Sunday, and the pastor told the
congregation that he and his family had taken a day trip to the
Manheim area to go to the fair. My mind got caught up in his story,
and this poem came out of it. This is a refreshing change from some of
the heaviness.

Something Different
Off to the fair to have some fun,
A change of pace for the day
My wife and I and our two sons
"Let's do something different", she called to say.

So over to Manheim, place of the fair,
The four of us started to roam:
Me and my wife and the boys planned to share
A trip to the place she called home.

"Let's look at the animals," shouted the boys,
Off went eight busy feet
"Too few animals here to enjoy"
Then to my surprise, an auction of sheep.

My message this Sunday before my eyes
As the auction was taking advance,
"Here's a good spot, hurry up you guys"
The sermon in my head had started to dance.

I watched the men, the thought on each face,
So important the sheep worth the cost,
And there in the center of that busy place
Was the poor little sheep, scared and lost.

Very dependent the nature of sheep
Near-sighted with no defense,
Range of vision about 45 feet
And rather short on animal sense.

I thought of the Shepherd, wise and good,
And knowing how to lead
Searching out the place of food
And showing the sheep where to feed.

I saw the Shepherd consider His sheep
Each one distinct, not the same.
Yes, they are dumb, still they will come
When His voice calls each by its name.

Born one day the Savior, Shepherd of the sheep
Who gave freely His life to bring.
Salvation and guidance, and promise to keep
The sheep of the Shepherd King.

DECEMBER 9, 1986

The Arid Place
My plants aren't getting watered,
My books aren't being read;
At night I write my poems
While tossing in my bed.

I'm feeling so frustrated
And I am all alone;
My inners can't find peace
My heart beats with a groan.

Work is going fine,

I'm soon to be promoted,
But with all this sighin'
You'd think I'd been demoted.

Mothering days are past,
No longer do I "wife";
How long Lord can I last
In this dry place in life?

Fill me from your watering can
Lord, come and fill me up,
And all that you have filled me with
Pour from out my cup.

"For I will pour water upon him who is thirsty, and
floods upon the dry land; I will pour my Spirit upon
your offspring, and my blessing upon your
descendants' (King James Version, Isa. 44.3)."

December 14, 1986

"'The grass withereth, the flower fadeth: because
the spirit of the Lord bloweth upon it' (King James
Version, Isa. 40:7)."

December 21, 1986

Drugstore Band-Aids
I have such a hurt
Deep inside today;
It's the kind of hurt
That won't quickly go away.

It's a crushing feeling:
A heavy kind of pain
That drags around my feet
And reaches 'round my brain.

Useless are my hands,

No sleep comes to my eyes;
My sometimes- steady breathing
Has increased to burden size...

Burdened sighs.

Don't sell me drugstore Band-Aids,
Injections, nor a crutch,
For the feeling in my middle
Hurts me much too much.

An x-ray could not picture
Nor take the hurt away,
But if only I could sit with You
My wound might heal today.

We often try to cover up our hurts with a Band-Aid, which sometimes takes the form of excessive food or drink, exercise, sex, hobbies, a whole variety of activities; over-work, or constant sleeping. We've all done some, or all of these for a short period of time, but there is a danger in over-using any of them as a substitute for really seeking to take care of the issue.

We often do the same to others. "Here let me fix it really quickly, so you and I can both feel better", often not really listening, and being available as they share their pain. While it is not good to hang on to pain too long, and live a defeated life, it is also not good to expect someone to "get over it", as soon as we decide it is time.

Sometimes our pain is too much for others to bear, and so they turn a deaf ear to our cry. They may feel helpless or in pain themselves and are unable to listen and offer wise counsel. Don't give up. There is someone out there whom the Lord has provided for you to go to. Search until you find that someone to talk with.

JANUARY 8-9, 1987   This next poem is from the parable in the Bible about the prodigal son; it is in Luke chapter 15. Both sons had access to all the father had. God, our father, does not play favorites, though it sometimes seems that way to us because we seem only able to see one side of what is going on, and we are on the wrong side!

The Prodigal
I'm so anxious to get home –
One more mile, and I'll arrive.
I wonder where he is right now –
Or if he's still alive.

I hope he'll recognize me
When I get to the door.
My clothes are torn, my sandals worn,
And I'm thinner than before.

Someone's coming in the distance –
Running very fast toward me –
Arms outreached and waving
Why, it's Papa's face I see!

Oh my, he's holding me so close;
Now he's looking in my face.
Is he wondering about my life
In that distant foreign place?

Dear Papa, can I tell you
How I've hungered in that land
And often had to beg for food
From out a stranger's hand?

How quickly I have wasted
The fortune for me saved
On pleasures most unworthy
Of the price we've had to pay?

Why Papa, you are smiling
In the tears that run with mine,
And as we sit together
Your tears drop in my wine.

My ears still seem to hear your shout
To servants 'round
"Bring the robe, prepare the feast

My son, at last, is found!"

These gifts are so magnificent,
For me who brought disgrace,
And Papa all you want to do
Is sweetly kiss my face.

I don't deserve this welcome –
The look inside your eyes –
A reflection of the son you love
Is what I realize.

You knew me when I walked afar,
You left me not alone.
My papa met me in the way
And walked with me back home.

If you have a parent who you are at odds with; even a broken relationship; try to mend it. Don't wait until it is too late, and then be filled with regret.

JANUARY 13, 1987

Early Dawn Glow
If you came to my home –
And I wish you would
I'd open up and spill me out –
If I only could.

If you came to my home
You'd have your pick of chairs;
We could talk, or take a walk,
To almost anywhere.

I could show you things I save –
Some can make me weep.
I'd love to show you the secret place
Where all my poems I keep.

And if I had the courage
And fear was not my guide
I, unheard, without a word,
Would sit down by your side.

I'd be the soul of a baby
Who long ago had been
Open wide, no need to hide
On my face what is within.

There'd be no time nor distance;
No hiding - not a trace.
You could see the who that's me
If you looked in my face.

I long to walk with someone
Where each could recognize
The other in the garden
Of pure un-shaded eyes.

I would not use a bunch of words
On which I now depend;
I'd hug you close and leave you know
You are my dearest friend.

It's fear that pulls the shades down tight
And fear that makes me hide.
It's fear that love in battle fights
To see me safe outside.

Love pushes through the darkness
And glows in early dawn –
Needs a face to embrace,
And searches for a home.

I think, perhaps, the only place to experience this may be in
the presence of the Lord. It is sad that I often find myself too busy to
devote the time to experiencing this.

Pained Love
Martyrs felt suffering pain –
Did they feel love more –
Do you think their pain began
When love knocked on their door?

Jesus, too, felt pain in depth
Because His love was great
And asked Him to absorb our sin
And from love separate.

Do you think love worth the cost
When pain comes in full measure?
It seems to me, when one loves,
It's pain that is the treasure.

I think the two synonymous:
Side-by-side they live.
Though love seems best when put to test,
It's pain love seems to give.

Do we decide to love
With heart or with the head?
When begun with either one
Pain and love are wed.

Is it love that wills, or the will that loves –
Which one gives the start?
Which goes on forever?
Which decides the heart?

Does love feel, or simply kneel
With love before the cross?
Is great pain less if on His breast?
It's love that counts the cost.
Why decide to love –
What reward is there to gain –

If to live is to give and yet, in return,
The gift we receive is pain?

APRIL 12, 1987   I watched a television movie on the
Holocaust, forcing myself to keep my eyes open through all the horrific
scenes. People can be so unbelievable cruel. I couldn't help but sob as
I watched it. Then I wrote the following poem. At the end I realized
how much hate I had in my heart for those who tortured the Jewish
people, which led me to realize, as well, that we are all capable of
horrible acts under certain circumstances. We all need the Savior.

Murderous Cry

Up from my depths
Comes a murderous cry
When I see the smoke
Of the Jews in the sky.

Reduced to one
Of the barbarous men
Who slaughtered the helpless –
So could I do to them.

Split I with hate
As they split up those loved
I envision the smoke
Of my hate rise above.

In my heart
I carry a whip like the man
Who beat them for pleasure
With the whip in his hand.

Murderous men
Of the Holocaust,
Love's shadow hangs o'er us
Here at the cross.

MAY 1987

Mighty Oak

the personification of a tree

Walking through the woods one day,
With a sack of fear,
I met a mighty oak
Who bade me to come here.

He said, "I've watched you come and go
In this woods for many a mile.
Why you carry that heavy load?"
He asked me with a smile.

I opened up my pack
And took a look inside –
When I thought I had the answer
Again my pack I tied.

"It follows me, it's part of me,
It comes with me", I said.
And then the mighty Oak
Shook his mighty head.

I watched him ruffle up his leaves,
Engage a dance with the breeze,
And then he stretched his arms above,
And offered an exchange of love.

"Exchange of love - what is that?!"
As I held to the fear inside my pack.

The oak tree gave me no answer –
It seemed I was all alone.
On that day when he looked away
I knew not that love he had sown.

Back and forth I traveled,
Often stopping near the tree.
There we'd sit and listen –
My heavy pack and me.

Once when I was out of sight,
A little late, you see,
I heard a love song in the night
Coming from the tree.

"Love is good, love is long,
Love can bend, for love is strong.
Love is brave, and also warm,
Love is safe, in many a storm.

Love has laughter, love sheds tears,
Love can wash away your fears.
Love wraps 'round, love leaves go,
Love is patient, and love does grow."

I grabbed my heavy pack
And hurried 'round the bend
Just in time to hear him sing
"Love will never end."

Then he stood up straight and tall,
"I've something to say", he said.
The fear in me made me feel small
So, in my pack, I stuck my head.

"You still carrying that old stuff around?",
As if he couldn't tell,
When I began to notice
In my pack a putrid smell.

"You need to empty out that pack —
There's no need to hide.
Get that burden off your back
And love will grow inside."

I brought my head out in the air
And looked up at the tree.
I asked him once again of love
But he just looked at me.

Then without warning in the night
There came a raging storm.
I stayed beside my friend the Oak
And I felt safe and warm.

Within the branches of his hold,
In the stormy wood,
I rested in a tender fold
And knew a feeling good.

When morning came I lifted my pack,
Wishing my journey would end.
I gave the mighty Oak a hug
And noticed that he could bend.

One day I asked my friend the Oak
Where he got his strength;
He pointed to a river
That seemed to have no length.

I saw his roots went down real deep
Into the river's side.
"This is where I get my strength
And how I'm satisfied."

I sat down by the river bank,
There beside the tree,
And opened up my heavy pack
That burdened fear in me.

I watched the river flow
And saw it not look back;
Then, surely as I could,
I emptied out my sack.

On and on it took my fear,
Away from out of sight.
There beside the mighty Oak,
I found my burden light.

I stayed along the river bank,
Underneath the tree,
My pack now full with the exchange
Of love that grew in me.

Sweet, tender love that onward moves
And spreads its healing balm,
I'll stay myself within your way,
And know love's quiet calm.

AUGUST 10, 1987

Today I was thinking how I never seem to have peace because of circumstances. Then the Lord showed me the only way to have peace is to accept it from the Lord. Otherwise I will never be able to attain it because I can't control all my circumstances. This is why I need His peace, and he wants to give it to me.

AUGUST 17-21, 1987

A Quest, A Song, A Show
the personification of a bird
I flew around the earth one day
Then searched the stars above.
I knew just what I wanted –
My quest was one for love.

Down into the valleys,
Up into the heights –
I read the many faces,
I searched in deepest nights.

I looked for love in the streets
While there among the crowd,
then I searched for love alone
And heard my heart wail loud.

"I gotta' get some love –
Some love I gotta' get!
Here comes someone who'll love me –

Love me best, I bet."

Flying high in his love
My heart could only sing,
Then the lover that I chose
Broke a needed wing.

Down I fell to the ground
And broke one of my feet.
How quickly love had brought me
Back upon the street.

One wing shattered, one foot broke,
My heart was sore perplexed.
I wondered in my search for love
What would happen next.

Then a thought occurred to me
While hovering 'neath my wing:
Perhaps I'll get some love
If I begin to sing.

"I gotta' have some love"
Was the song from night till dawn,
"I gotta', gotta' have some love!",
And so my song went on and on.

My voice was growing weak and frail
And I was in a state.
I hopped into a corner
And studied hard my fate.

If love is what I need,
And love is what I sought,
And if no one can give to me,
Perhaps it can be bought.

Within myself I formed a plan
So love-feed I could get.

I'll sell the very best of me
And I'll find love-feed yet.

I learned to do all kinds of tricks –
A show all of my own.
I sang and danced, and I romanced,
Yet still, I felt alone.

All day long I tried and tried
To get myself some feed –
Now, within my shattered heart,
I fast began to bleed.

Foolish little sparrow,
Clown upon the street,
Go back into you corner –
Your search for love has brought defeat.

And so I folded all myself
Inside a silent dream
And there within the darkness
I fashioned myself a dream.

He came walking down the street
Looking left and right.
He came into my corner,
His eyes had pierced my deepest night.

He wanted not a show,
Nor required of me a thing,
And before I made a sound,
He began to sing.

"I am the love that you have sought,
I am the bread you need.
The love I have cannot be bought
Yet needs to be received."
Then he picked me up
To nest within his hand,

And somewhere in my darkest hour
The healing touch of love began.

He fed me with his broken bread
And bound my injured wing.
My shattered heart he mended whole –
Again, my voice began to sing.

I slowly put aside my act
And laid my tricks to rest.
The song that grew inside of me
Was love sung at its best.

My wing began healing –
On one foot I could hop.
And there within his giant hand
My singing would not stop.

Then I awoke from out my dream
And, much to my surprise,
I lay within a well-worn hand
And looked into familiar eyes.

We walked around the streets that day –
Me inside his hand.
He showed me other sparrows
In every corner of his land.

"This one's hungry, this one's sad,
This one is dying, this one is mad.
This one's frightened, this one has lied.
Each one is the reason I came and died."

We walked the night in silence,
his eyes were fixed above.
I was safely in his hand,
Resting in the pulse of love.

Morning came - and, with a sigh,

I knew the time had come to fly.

He told me I'd be lonely
Yet never be alone.
He said his open, wounded hand
Would ever be my home.

I walked around the streets today,
I've felt the stars above
To search within dark corners
For someone needing love.

NOVEMBER 4, 1987

Fantasy
Down the cobbled-path I go
Over the bridge that well I know,
Into a land called "Fantasy"
And the man that is there waiting for me.

No matter which the path I choose
His face I always see;
And though no locks are in this land
Within his hand he holds the key.

We meet here face-to-face –
He's waiting as he said –
And over the bridge in Fantasy land
The man with the key and I are wed.

The clock slows down upon the wall,
Other voices hold their call,
And on my heart a gentle knock –
And the key in his hand turns its lock.

The key is of silver, the man of pure gold
And the color I am finds release in his hold.
We walk, and talk, and stillness flows
A sweetness lives and likeness grows.

I stay there a day and then some more,
And then I stay the years.
The man with the key, that unlocked my heart,
Had just come for a visit and left me in tears.

I'll awake one day and find him gone –
I'll search out and call his name.
And over the bridge in Fantasy land
I'll know I am alone again.

NOVEMBER 17, 1987   Divorce settled. The death of a dream. His;
Mine; Ours.

26
Peace amidst the Pieces

Following the divorce in November I felt a tremendous weight lift off me. I had lived 24 years never knowing when the police might show up at our door, when our name might be in the paper for wrongdoings, or even knowing about narrow escapes my husband had. I worried that our children might hear things in school. Our whole marriage I teetered on the sea-saw of reality versus fantasy; of partial trust versus deception. The most destruction came through lies. Lies that I no longer could tell if they were lies or truth. The discernment I once had was gone. Once trust is gone, it is like climbing a hill to the safety of home with a thousand-pound sack on your back. Lying comes from the father of lies, the enemy of God. It is one of the most destructive forces ever. I was constantly suspicious, and constantly reprimanding myself for not trusting.

Now, I had no reason to be suspicious, or fearful, at least for a time. It was a very freeing feeling.

However, I was not free of the feelings of failure on my part. I had tried to keep our family together hoping that each "incident" would be the last one; hoping that now we could be a happy family; hoping that all the bad stuff was over. Looking back, I think in some ways I was selfish. I did not want to admit that our marriage failed; for somehow that would make me a failure. I was also concerned in the early years with how I could support my children. I wanted them to have security, and a complete home. I believed that could only come about with both a mother and a father. I was worried what would happen to them without a father in their life. My desire to "fix" things came to naught, and now here we were! One teen married, one teen at home, and all the confusion, sadness, anger, and our reality to deal with.

I had become so used to constantly examining my motives for everything, constantly trying to figure myself out that I could not seem to stop. I was always guilty inside for something. I thought that if I took responsibility for everything I could then make everything okay. This thinking is not only unrealistic, but it also assumes power that only God has.

JUNE 21, 1987

Veiled
Here I am behind the veil
That seeks to imprison me
And in this tiresome battle
There's no security.

Once more I'm standing in this place,
Pleading once again my case,
And though I am before your face,
I'm trapped behind a veil.

I feel like I'm before a judge:
I sit where I must swear.
The jury waits inside of me
Behind the veil we share.

I enter in a well-known plea
Of fear that's made a home in me.
The evidence is plain to see,
Here behind the veil.

Feelings seem to disappear
Inside the thinking that I hear
And courage bows its head in fear
Here inside the veil.

My mind is working overtime,
As though I'm guilty of some crime,
And I myself hide in rhyme
And break from out the veil.

I seem to lose the self of me
And find I have to "try to be"

And each time failure stares at me
Here inside the veil.

I sit, I watch, I listen well –
Here inside my homemade shell
Which feels much like a prison cell,
With me behind the veil.

My feelings hide as though asleep;
The search goes on within the deep;
And in despair I sometimes weep,
Alone behind the veil.

In 1 Corinthians the Apostle Paul writes:

But with me it is a very small thing that I should be
judged of you, or of man's judgment: yea, I judge not
mine own self. For I know nothing by myself; yet am
I not hereby justified: but he that judgeth me is the
Lord' (King James Version, 1 Cor. 4.4-5)."

There were many years following the divorce that continued
to be difficult for each of us, in different ways, and for different
reasons. I will let my grown children tell their story if they want to. If
they don't, I will respect their privacy but I want you to know that their
stories are every bit as traumatic and powerful as mine; and they were
only children when this all began. It left them with inner turmoil, and
at times they made poor choices that caused hurt to themselves and
those around them. A good reminder for all of is that where there is
ongoing sin in the life of one, it never affects only that one. It spreads
around, sometimes far and wide.
In 1987 I sold our home and bought a mobile, after which I
worked part time in both a sweater store, and a day care. Periodically I
would write short poems to put on my answering machine, or maybe
for Bible school, but not really anything too much in depth. At this
time in my life, my ex-husband and I were no longer communicating.
There was a period of time when our children and he were also not
speaking. It was during this time that I had a dream, and the only thing

in my dream was a verse in "Malachi." I woke up and did not know
what the verse was, so I looked it up.

> "'And he shall turn the heart of the fathers to the
> children, and the heart of the children to their
> fathers, lest I come and smite the earth with a curse'
> (King James Version, Mal. 4.6)."

It wasn't until many, many years later that once again their
father was back in their lives, in fact back in all of our lives. God's grace
continued, and so did His purpose, for His own reasons.

27
Day Care Babies

1987   I wrote this poem when working in a day care. Most parents have experienced the many sides to a baby.

Babies

Dear little babies, so clean and so sweet,
In fresh smelling clothes from head to their feet,
Tummies are full, Mom and Dad out the door.
Look out, caregivers! We're on the loose, once
more!

Dribble and drool is what we do best.
How'd that slime jump from my bib to my chest?

We roll and we crawl, tumble and fall;
Our favorite place is the floor.
They sit me up straight, oh dear it's too late –
My nose hit that same spot before!

I'm starting early my life of crime,
I'm crazy for pacifiers – they don't have to be mine.
You think yours is safe in your tight little grip.
Aha! Now I've got it in my two baby lips!

Yummy, dum, dum, and doodley doo.
Yours tastes much like mine, all covered with drool.

Now, it's my turn in the walker
And ya' better get outta' my way!
I'll run over your toes and smash your wee nose,
I'm the "Day Care Destroyer" today!

Oh no, it's that time again –
That annoying diaper brigade.
They always want to get to the bottom of things
And insist on changing what we've made!

Ho hum, the close of another day;
I best put on a sweet smile, for I'll soon be rescued
and home in my bed, I guess I've done another day
care in style.

For those of you who have worked in day care you can
appreciate how important it is to have each child's name on his/her
clothing, etc. Equally important is that each child has a cubby to put
said items in.

Cubby Clothes
I don't know who I belong to,
I'm lying in a cubby;
But whose body fits me?
Is it Suzie, Sally, or Stubby?

Please take me home and name me;
So if an accident occurs,
Your little boy won't be embarrassed
By wearing one of hers!

And then, of course, there is nap time, with those ever lovin'
pillows!

Pillow Talk
They may look fluffy and might look cool,
But pillows as well get covered with drool.
Yucky yuck yuck, and slobbery goo.
Please take me home before they use me for glue!

Another Day at Care Day
Morning brings to us again
Faces clean and bright;
Ten little toddlers

That we sent home last night.

Chubby little feet
With chubby little toes,
And upon each little face
A little, chubby nose.

The chatter begins,
Toys cover the floor;
The gate is in place
At toddler room door.

Now it's time for diaper check,
We dare not miss one bun;
So up on the table, a fresh one in place,
The Pamper Parade Replacement is done.

Snack time is here, and then out to pay,
"Please Mr. Sunshine, we need you today".
On go the coats, the hats and the mittenS,
Off in a hurry are ten toddler kittens.

Some are on rides,
Some play with balls,
Some down the slide,
Released from four walls.

Now the time for rest is here,
A moment in the pen;
We'll give a book to each of you,
Then lift you out again.

A bib beneath each waiting chin,
Securely in its place;
A small, white spoon for every hand
Will find its way to toddler face.

We feed them and wash them,
And bed them for nap;

And often read stories
On "too small a lap"!

We sing and we dance,
Cuddle and rock;
Teach them to help
As we pick up each block.

The day is coming to an end,
And slowly each child goes;
Tomorrow is another day
In which your toddler quickly grows.

The room is all quiet,
Toys neatly in their places;
But one thing is missing:
Ten toddler sweet faces!

It is true that the little ones are very sweet, impressionable, and needy. I've worked through the years in a couple of day cares, and most caretakers are kind, but overworked. Teachers often have to deal with children who have a variety of behavioral problems. Patience does wear thin, as does energy. Sometimes this is the only choice parents have, because neither spouse makes enough to support the family, and harder still is the single parent who desires to be home with their little one, but is sole support, and just not able to be. Then there are other parents who simply want to have a child, but be away from that child as much as possible, out of preference. I guess I would challenge all parents to consider what children may experience adversely from being in day care, but are unable to express.

2015   Below is another daycare poem written from the perspective of a small child who is not having the best of time under the supervision of one who possibly is in the wrong line of work.

Day Care Disaster
Early in the morning
At dawn of every day

They drop me off at this place
Where I'm supposed to stay.

Eight or nine hours later
When the day is done
They pick me up and take me home,
Supposing I had fun!

They don't know, cause I can't tell them
"She" hollered most of the day,
Unless I did just what she said,
Exactly on time, and just her way.

I cried, I hit, and sometimes bit,
She said that I did bad!
But no one ever cared enough,
To see I just felt sad.

I had to eat without a spill,
Or my food would be thrown away;
And then I had to be real still
For nap time was part of the day.

I seldom heard a kind sweet word
From start of day till done
I almost forgot but it means a lot
To tell you I was only one.

Now that I am two and I'm in another class,
Perhaps it is different but I know it is true,
That I'm one of a growing mass.

I'd better be trained,
I'd better be cute,
I'd better be smart,
And well-behaved, to boot!

But what if I'm not,
Can't measure up

Too shy or too sissy,
Too rough and too tough.
Well there is always the chair
I'm used to sitting there!

I've made it to three
And can express myself well,
But there's no one to listen,
And I've no one to tell

That just by being here,
I'm one of the bunch;
Seldom home at breakfast time,
And never home for lunch.

Mommy is tired
At the end of her day
Daddy is weary
And turns his ears the other way.

I'm feeling sad
As I sit on the floor
And I think to myself
Next week I'll be four.

Four, and I've almost made it,
One more year to go;
I wonder why my belly hurts,
And why I don't seem to grow.

I've learned to be so very neat,
I never soil my pants,
I've learned to do just as she says
I've learned to do the Day Care Dance.

And now I am five
And I look in the nursery
And see those sweet babies there,
Dropped off at dawn,

Still asleep with a yawn
And I wonder, does anyone care?

But we have money in the bank,
And we have nice clothes to wear,
Because five of my years
I spent in day care...

Helping to get my parents there!

28
A Flower is Born in the Desert

JANUARY 1, 1988   From my journal: Every life has a reason.

Aftermath
As I lay upon my bed,
My tears flow out in silent dread,
No one here to see them roll,
The crushed felt feeling of my soul.

JANUARY 2, 1988   From my journal: If I only touch His garment, I shall be restored to health.

JANUARY 27, 1988   We say we have faith for salvation, yet we lack it for daily bread.

FEBRUARY 25, 1988   We should not make provisions for the flesh, by feeding it what it likes. It is supposed to be dead, so we shouldn't try to keep it alive. We are not to "pit" ourselves against the Holy Spirit, but yield to him.

MARCH 1988

The King Dies
The king fell off his throne
And landed on his head;
Where once he ruled within my heart,
Now the king is dead.

But God, the true King, remains alive forever. He has no beginning and no ending. He always was, and always will be.

MARCH 1988

A very special event took place this month; a happy event. My first grandchild was born. A little girl. I wrote a couple of poems for her. Here are three of them which were read at her baby shower.

At the time I am writing this book, my baby granddaughter is a young married woman with two little boys, and a third baby on the way.

Greetings
Hello everyone, my name is Harmony.
I'm so happy you've come to party with me.
I'll try to visit all around and greet you everyone
So we can share together a little party fun.

Maybe you can hold me and listen to me coo
For I'm a bit too tiny to big girl talk with you.
Thank-you for the lovely gifts - you've been so kind, I
see!
Now on with the shower, on with the fun, its' time to
party with me!

A Little Problem
I have a little problem - my hair is falling out!
It's a little bit perplexing, as you can guess, no doubt.
Sometimes new folks think I'm a boy or else they try
to guess.
Do you think that my attire need always be a dress?

One day I will surprise them when this little fuzz you
see
Will grow up there, and then my hair will show them
I'm a she!

Harmony's Present From God
He gave me two eyes, a mouth, and a nose,
Ten tiny fingers, and ten mini toes,
a heart of my own to go with my mind,
Ears, knees and elbows - all the right kind.

He gave me some friends - you, sitting here –

And picked out my birth date: the time and the year,
A brand-new mommy and daddy and home
And even some "fuzz" to cover my dome.

Before I ever heard it, before I ever came,
Even then He loved me - already knew my name.
Don't you think that's special - I "wriggle" up with
glee
For before I ever came to earth He gave these lovely
gifts to me.

APRIL 18, 1988   For my son:

"'I will be his Father, and he shall be My son: and I
will not take My mercy and steadfast love away from
him' (King James Version, 1 Chron. 17.13)."

MAY 14, 1988   From my journal: As I woke up this morning,
I was singing "Bind us together, Lord, bind us together." I had been
singing it in my sleep.

JUNE 19, 1988   On Fathers' day, my father told me he
sometimes recites scripture before he falls asleep. His favorite verse is

"'And we know that all things work together for
good to them who are the called according to His
purpose' (King James Version, Rom. 8:28)."

29
Desert Hunger

1989   During this year my father and son
unexpectedly had to take me to the emergency room because all of a
sudden one evening I was freezing cold, though it wasn't cold in my
home; I also could barely stand; I was very weak. In the emergency
room I was diagnosed with depression. I had recently begun to see a
different counselor and she asked me if my doctor had checked my
thyroid, which he hadn't. I made an appointment with him, and after
blood work found out that my thyroid was barely working. He put me
on medicine, and while I won't say there had been no depression,
once the thyroid medicine kicked in, I did start to feel better.

FEBRUARY 15, 1989

Crumbs
I don't even know what to ask for,
I don't even know what I need.
I only ask you to fill me, Lord,
Or give me some crumbs on which to feed.

Touched
There's a kind of weeping
That's only done apart
When the written word or music heard
Touches deep the heart.

FEBRUARY 28, 1989

Gone
The years have disappeared before my very eyes.
Gone are the days of wonder and surprise.
Though jaded, they faded, and left me filled

With long and hungry sighs.

I was now 48, and my son had left for college, and my daughter had already been married four years, and had an 11-month-old little girl, and another on the way.

I, myself would experience loneliness, and yet often it was combined with feelings of gratitude because my life was much less tumultuous.

Did I miss my husband? Of course, I did. As I think about it now I realize he fed me what I lacked. He helped me feel good about myself, and I needed that. He appreciated how I kept our home; he appreciated my abilities; he liked my cooking; he liked that I enjoyed having people into our home; he liked that I was intelligent, and he liked that we could have fun together. We had shared many common interest including our children.

There was a vacant hole in my heart that wasn't filled. I often wondered, "Could the Lord really fill this spot?"

JUNE 1989

Faces
This week He came to me
In faces that I knew –
In the outstretched arms of friends,
And in a stranger, too.

How grateful I was for my friends.

JULY 14, 1989

Not a Friend, But...
Not a friend but a Father
Who'd fill my cup within,
With food and drink and nourishment –
Overflow the brim.

Not a friend but a mother
Who'd pat and hold and stroke
The bruised child inside of me,

And parts that had been broke.

Not a friend, but a lover.

Not a friend, but a Savior
Who'd seek and wait and find,
Who'd lead and walk the path with me,
And sit with me and dine.

And He is doing this; I just often don't recognize so.

July 16, 1989, 5:57 a.m.

Stuffing
Stuffing or filling, as its sometimes called,
Is loved by some, enjoyed by most –
But when I'm the turkey that's getting fat –
The stuffing I use ain't where it's at!

July 17, 1989, 11:20 p.m.

Honesty
When I no longer care how people think about me,
then I begin responding more honestly.

Caring about what people think of us can be a bondage if what they
think means too much, and causes us to pretend.

July 18, 1989, 6:30 a.m.

My Dream
I also have a dream,
Dr. Martin Luther King.

It may not be as far and wide,
And not the world improve,
Does not promote equality
So black and white can move

Within the same perimeter
And notice not the race.
It's hidden in my heart
And veiled upon my face.

It will not span the ages,
Nor be engraved in stone.
You had a dream for thousands,
And mine is just my own.

"'What other nation is so great as to have their gods
near them the way the Lord our God is near us
whenever we pray to Him? And what other nation is
so great as to have such righteous decrees and laws
as this body of laws I am setting before you today?
Only be careful, and watch yourselves closely so that
you do not forget the things your eyes have seen or
let them slip from your heart as long as you live.
Teach them to your children and to their children
after them' (New International Version, Deut. 4.7-
9)."

July 19, 1989 8:06 A.M.

Shifting Gears
When people come near I shift into another gear.
I go inside - feel a need to hide.
The words that I feed apply to their need,
And yet I can see my emotions are me.

And though I'm protected, because I'm unseen,
And seldom rejected, I need to be weaned
From the bottle I was fed with formula untrue
That the hiding of myself should be what pleases
you.

I have grown up covering irritations with great zeal and trying
to protect us all from emotions that I feel. This is why I often
preferred being alone; I could breathe. And yet I also found joy in

being with friends. I guess these are some of the incongruities of an introvert.

July 19, 1989 10:15 p.m.

Silent Sound
There's a kind of weeping
That's only done apart;
When the written word, Or the music heard,
Touches deep the heart.

Reflections
Pencil in hand;
The sound of a band;
Money to pay the bills.

A baby at birth;
A dry kind of mirth;
And music that gives me a thrill.

Planning the fun
When dinner is done
For people who come to my home.

A walk in the park,
The quiet of dark,
And time to reflect when alone.

August 13, 1989   Develop Your plans, Lord.

"'But they hastily forgot His works; they did not wait for His plans respecting them' (Amplified, Ps. 106.13)."

In August of 1989 it was with joy my second granddaughter was born. Two adorable little girls, and a visit to Foofoo's house, (which is what the oldest, at 18 months old, dubbed me), prompted this next poem. I found out many years later that the word "Foofoo" is a staple food in many countries in Africa.

Foofoo's House

The house of Foofoo on a choice weekday morn
Takes on a baby's artistic kind of form.
Most usually neat and quiet too
These four tiny feet turn it into a zoo!

Toys find their way from behind cupboard door,
Free for the day upon Foofoo floor.
Out on the patio colored chalk in design
Pink, blue and yellow form squiggly line.

Muffin is running as fast as can be,
Calling to mommy to come and "watch me"!
Puddie creeps off her blanketed place,
And feathery grass brings a smile to her face.

Nap time approaches and babies are fed;
A bottle prepared, a story is read.
Lunch finds it home in out-of-way places,
As well as across two sweet baby faces.

Finally settled; not a peep, not a sound;
All is now peaceful in Foofoo house town.
Out comes the Scrabble, it's our turn to play;
You've now had a visit to Foofoo's today.

30
Hope in the Desert

This year I finally found the job I was most fulfilled in. I began working as an activity aide in a local nursing home. It provided me opportunity to be creative in many ways. It provided the opportunity to encourage lonely and hurting residents, and for eight hours a day take my focus off the emotional pain I felt in my heart.

It was the first job I had, outside my home, that gave me the fulfillment I needed. I remained there four years which was an all-time record for me.

FEBRUARY 16, 1990   Gentleman's Psalm. To Jeff, Dana, and all males who enter this family from this time forth. Love, Mom.

> "'He who walks and lives uprightly and blamelessly, who works rightness and justice, and speaks and thinks the truth in his heart. He who does not slander with his tongue, nor does evil to his friend, not takes up a reproach against his neighbor. In whose eyes a vile person is despised, but he honors those who fear the Lord-who revere and worship Him; who swears to his own hurt and does not change; He who does not put out his money for interest (to one of his own people) and who will not take a bribe against the innocent. He who does these things shall never be moved' (Amplified, Ps. 15.2-5)."

AUGUST 19, 1990   This morning when I woke up this thought came to me: Sometimes we spend our whole lives trying to please everyone because when we were little there was one person we felt we couldn't please. Then as adults we become angry when we find someone else we can't please even though we try very hard to do so.

SEPTEMBER 25, 1990   Upon reading the verses below, I wrote the poem that follows them.

"'Thy people shall be willing in the day of thy power, in the beauties of holiness from the womb of the morning: thou hast the dew of thy youth' (King James Version, Ps. 110:3)."

"'Wherefore he saith, awake thou that sleepest, and arise from the dead, and Christ shall give thee light' (King James Version, Eph. 5.14)."

"'In the beauties of holiness from the womb of the morning: thou hast the dew of thy youth' (King James Version, Ps. 110: 3 (I certainly did not feel like I had the dew of my youth, but the words "womb of the morning" held a promise of a new day.)

SEPTEMBER 1990

Womb of the Morning
Out of the womb of the morning
Comes another new day,
Be it sun-filled or snowing,
Or a dull shade of gray,

Giving birth to some newness,
Unseen the day before,
Finding reason to praise
Since the last 24.

Drink of the water, awake from your sleep,
Raise up your hands, sow now, then reap.
It's the day of His power, and in holy array,
From the womb of the morning,
He gives another new day.

31
Ripening of the Desert Fruit

1991   The year is now 1991, and my adult children
are struggling with difficult issues. That is such a simple statement but
it is packed full of their pain, turmoil, poor choices, and consequences
that I wish not to share out of respect for their privacy. It, however,
needs to be acknowledged because "in the beginning" they were
birthed into our family, and through no fault of their own they became
part of our unhealthy marriage. We all leave a legacy of some sort. It is
never too late to build a good one; the house upon the Rock. God, the
Rock, is faithful during more years in the desert for us all.

God is never, ever finished with our growth; He is ever
seeking to conform us to the likeness of Jesus. My peace comes from
the truth that God is able, and willing to use anything in our lives for
good that we turn over to Him. I have utmost confidence in the desires
of both my son and daughter that will enable Him to continue to do
this. He is the Master Artist, Carpenter, and Completer of His work.

JANUARY 30, 1991   I had a dream last night, and I was singing
"Man of Sorrows". I sang 4 verses in my dream.

Foot of the Cross
At the foot of the cross,
With my face to the ground,
Something splashed o'er me
And circled around.

At first I hardly noticed
From where the dripping came,
Yet I heard someone calling,
Calling out my name.

Up I looked and saw a man

Upon a wooden tree,
I wondered why, with each heaving sigh,
His life's blood fell on me.

He hung upon that wooden cross
In my heart, year after year,
And, in His wondrous mercy,
He kept me staying near.

Sometimes I'd look up at Him,
Yet slow to realize,
That he was pouring out His blood
Upon my blinded eyes.

Once He spoke to my heart and said,
"Child, turn your head
And I will drop my precious blood
Upon your ears that are dead."

Down his blood poured
And high his blood rose
And out of his side,
His heart of love flowed.

Jesus was His name,
My Savior on a tree.
He made his blood a river of love
To cleanse and purify me.

In 1991 as I was recuperating from an operation gone awry, and while my eyes were closed I imagined I was dancing with Jesus.

While My Eyes Were Closed, His Arms Were Open
I closed my eyes,
Enjoying the music I was listening to.
Suddenly, in my mind's eye,
I found myself in a room as vast as space;

The floor beneath my unclad feet was gold – pure
gold – unlike anything I've ever seen.
I was wearing a white gossamer dress and it fell
softly in points around my ankles.

It was plain and lovely.

And this!

This, the most wondrous thing that has ever
happened to me, happened next.
I looked up and I saw Him –
I saw Him inviting me to dance.

I saw His face and He was wonderfully laughing –
wonderful delight,
Him – wonderful sight – and we danced.

Dance with me Jesus, Jesu, Lover of my soul.

I danced with Him,
He danced with me,
And, in His wondrous, wondrous laugh,
Was the victory dance of all eternity.

32
Nightmares in The Desert

AUGUST 25, 1991   I had a dream where these three words were in my mind; "Ani", "Ali", "Amni". Only this week as I am writing this was I able to look up these words. I could not find the last word. The other two are associated with 911. Help! Curious. Of course, had no I phone or computer at that time to search out the meanings.

FEBRUARY 7, 1991   Last night I had a frightening dream, and I believe the enemy is trying to scare me because I am praying for my ex-husband. In my dream I was on the first floor of an enormous two-story house. My mother, and someone else were on the second story, to the left.

   I was being attacked by demons and they kept trying to smother me. I was screaming with all my might but there was another noise in the house, and my mother couldn't hear me.

   Then I ran out into the middle of the downstairs entry way, screaming. It was a massive room with wide steps going to a second floor. Something large and white was trying to cover my mouth. Suddenly at the top of the stairs from the middle room came Satan. He was dressed in black, and had a black beard. He was furious and came running down the stairs. I kept screaming in my sleep to him that the power of the blood of Jesus was stronger than he was. I woke up and my mouth was wide open, and I felt very frightened for myself and my family.

FEBRUARY 27, 1991   Everywhere I look my life is stressed; except UP.

FEBRUARY 28, 1991   I had such a nightmare last night where I was being terrorized by Satan. He was pulling me, beyond my own strength, into a room that was dark, and filled with old furniture. On the door of the room was a picture with his face on it. We were struggling and as I woke up I was mumbling in a deep voice that God is good! During the dream that is what the struggle was, in part, about. I kept pleading the power of the blood of Jesus, and to calm myself when I awoke, I continued to say to the enemy that "God is Good", and continued to plead the power of the blood of Jesus.

APRIL 10,1991   Drained; so weary.

> "'O Lord, you have heard the desire and longing of
> the humble and oppressed; You will prepare and
> strengthen and direct their heart, you will cause your
> ear to hear, to do justice to the fatherless and the
> oppressed, so that man who is of the earth may not
> terrify them anymore' (King James Version, Ps. 10:17
> and 18)."

APRIL 15, 1991   Scraping bottom; discouraged.

MAY 1, 1991   Last night I had a dream about a bear. In this one I was outside with two older women and a man. All of a sudden a bear came out of the woods and started running towards us. I ran in the house and so did an elderly lady. I got free but the bear began biting the older woman as she crouched upon the bed.
I few weeks ago I had a dream about a bear coming into a house where my children and I lived. It entered my son's room. I climbed out a window in order to come back in the front door, and divert its attention. It was a very frightening dream.

MAY 1, 1991   My daughter is so, so depressed over all she is remembering. O Lord!

MAY 2, 1991   Thank you Lord for the sunshine of today. There is something about sunshine that brings hope into view once more.

MAY 6, 1991   Harmony (three) calls me "Honey" sometimes. Isn't that so sweet! Charity (one and a half) has the dearest little expressions on her face. These little girls make me want to start over.

MAY 7, 1991   I feel so blah; almost nothing interests me. I am so down; I feel like I will never get above ground again. I feel like my whole life I've done nothing but struggle to survive. My worth has always been in being needed. My strength has always come when I needed to be strong for someone else. When I need to be strong for me, I can't be. I don't know how. I went to the doctor's today because my throat and tongue have been sore. He couldn't find anything wrong. He did, however, do a blood test again for thyroid, and cholesterol.

My blood pressure was up to 160/96. I still don't want to go on medicine. He told me to lose 10 pounds.

JUNE 19, 1991   I don't know why but the Lord brought the verse in Matthew to my mind while I was praying. Here is what it says:

> "'Blessed are the peace makers for they shall be called the sons of God' (King James Version, Matt. 5.9)."

JUNE 20, 1991   While sleeping the Lord brought this verse to me.

> "'I can do all things through Christ who strengthens me' (New King James Version, Phil. 4.13)."

JULY 10, 1991   This morning I cried; cried out my broken heart to the Lord. I cried for my children and myself to be released from all this pain. I cried about my finances; my job where I don't make enough money; and my loneliness. I cried because I don't feel well anymore. I cried and asked the Lord to bring my son a steak. I cried because it has been a long time since I have been able to fill our refrigerator with food. I cried because my needs are so many and I overlook seeking the Lord for Himself.
The Lord spoke to my heart and said,

> "'Call unto me and I will answer thee and show thee great and mighty things which thou knowest not' (King James Version, Jer. 33.3)."

He asked me to trust Him to meet my needs, to set me free.

"'Behold, (in the future restored Jerusalem),'my
family', I will lay upon it health and healing, and I will
cure them and will reveal to them the abundance of
peace, prosperity, security, stability, and truth'
(Amplified, Jer. 33.6)."

I clung to verses in God's word to get me from one moment
to the next. I would not have survived except that He was always with
me. I was horribly depressed.

JULY 18, 1991   I had an awful dream last night. I was home
alone in our home, and my ex-husband's dad came and was looking
for something in the brown station wagon. That was the car that was
given to us after he died. His eyes looked awful, dark, like death. I was
afraid of him. I began ordering him to leave by using the power and
blood of Jesus's name. He kept coming, and as he got closer and closer
he looked more and more like Satan. Soon he was attacking me and I
had to keep wiping blood from my eyes. He was very powerful, and I
seemed to be losing the battle. I kept telling him that the Lord was the
Victor, and no matter what he did to me, the Lord was still, in the end,
going to win the battle. Then he stuck something in my mouth, and I
bit down hard on it. It was the tail of a snake. Then I woke up; it was
1.55 a.m.

AUGUST 4, 1991

"'It is time for the Lord to act' (Amplified, Ps.
119:126)."

AUGUST 5, 1991   When I came home from work today I took
a nap. I had a dream about a man named Lloyd, who lived in
Huntsville. I had no idea who he was, but I prayed for his healing. I
often prayed for him through many years, and every once in a very
great while, he comes to mind, and I still do.

AUGUST 9, 1991   Last night I had a dream about a woman
who put her hand in a small paper bag where she had two cents. For

some reason, she had to have the bag torn open in order to get her hand out. During this time she said, "I surrender all". I woke myself up singing that hymn.

I don't know where I heard this statement but it gives food for thought. "Sometimes God makes us a prisoner of circumstances in life to teach us how to be free inside".

"'Like clay in the hand of the potter, so are you in my hand' (New International Version, Jer. 18:6)."

AUGUST 1991

On the Potter's Wheel
I wonder what He is doing,
What He is making of me.
Mostly I don't know,
And mostly I can't see.

But every once in a while,
He'll remove the scales that blind,
And then in that wondrous moment
He'll show me what's in His mind.

He'll speak in a word or two,
What He wants me to hear,
And then He returns to the work in his hands,
An oddly formed lump of clay.

With patient persistent direction,
He works on it day after day;
Clay that is cracked, worn, and hardened,
And set within its way.

His hands continue their molding
And shaping it year after year;
And the clay becomes the dream in His heart
As He softens it with His tears.

SEPTEMBER 1991

"'He who heeds instruction and correction is (not only himself) in the way of life, but is a way of life for others. And he who neglects or refuses reproof (not only himself) goes astray, but causes to err and is a path toward ruin for others' (Amplified, Prov. 10.17)."

DECEMBER 26, 1991

"'For though the Lord is high, yet has He respect to the lowly (bringing them into fellowship with Him)' (Amplified, Ps. 138.6)."

Though you, Lord, are perfectly stable, you care about me, and will allow me to know you as I allow you to know me.

33
Desert Life Continues

"'But only with God is (perfect) wisdom and might:
He alone has (true) counsel and understanding'
(Amplified, Job 12.13)."

In July of 1992, my son was on a mission trip to Jamaica, and he called and gave me the following verse to read.

"'If you have raced with men on foot and they have
tired you out, then how can you compete with
horses: And if you take flight in a land of peace
where you feel secure, then what will you do (when
you tread the tangled maze of jungle, haunted by
lions) in the swelling of the Jordan' (Amplified, Jer.
12.5)."

My heart is touched by people who raise their hands in worship.

NOVEMBER 30, 1992

"'Come to Me, all you who labor and are heavy-
laden and over-burdened, and I will cause you to
rest; I will ease and relieve and refresh your souls'
(Amplified, Matt. 11.28)."

JUNE 6, 1993   For my children:

"'He who earnestly seeks after and craves
righteousness, mercy and loving-kindness will find

197

life in addition to righteousness (uprightness and right standing with God) and also honor' (Amplified, Prov. 21.21)."

For the next eight years I wrote only two poems; one was for parents who had lost their baby, and the other four lines of my silent cries. There continued to be much to deal with in our family. My daughter was dealing with Chrones disease; I had a lengthy bout with hives, and other female problems; and my son had very difficult things that he continued to work through. Just because the marriage was over, that did not automatically take care of all the after effects.

I've included some verses, and a few things from a journal, but I have no record of any poem written until 1996. At this time in my life, I was reading from the Amplified Bible, so the verses are taken from it.

FEBRUARY 13, 1994   Sunday evening and I feel so discouraged. My daughter said she is so very tired. She was turned down for health insurance because of the pre-existing Chrones. My son's car left him sit in Waynesboro last night, and he needs 600.00 to have it fixed. We all are discouraged tonight.
MARCH 6, 1994

"'In Your faithfulness answer me, and in Your righteousness' (Amplified, Ps. 143.1b)."

April 4, 1994

"'Why go I mourning because of the oppression of the enemy' (Amplified, Ps. 42.9b)?"

"'Why are you cast down, O my inner self? And why should you moan over me and be disquieted within me? Hope in God and wait expectantly for Him; for I shall yet praise Him Who is the help of my countenance, and my God' (Amplified, Ps. 42.11)."

May 29, 1994

"'Blessed be God, who has not rejected my prayer, nor removed His mercy and loving-kindness from being with me' (Amplified, Ps. 66.20)."

And His mercy and loving-kindness is always with me.

JULY 10, 1994

"'When the Lord has given you rest from your sorrow and pain, and from your trouble and un- rest, and from the hard service with which you were made to serve, you shall say, "how the oppressor is stilled"' (Amplified, Isa. 14.3)."

OCTOBER 7, 1994

"'Blessed be the Lord God, the God of Israel, who alone does wondrous things' (Amplified, Ps. 72.18)."

OCTOBER 22, 1994

"'The Lord takes pleasure in those who reverently worshipfully fear Him, in those who hope in His mercy and loving-kindness. He makes peace in your borders' (Amplified, Ps. 147.11 and 14a)."

And He does that years later.
The Lord God was always walking with me. I took great strength and hope from His Word, but I did not always sense His presence. It is so easy to focus on the problem rather than the Problem-Solver.

JANUARY 3, 1995

"'Hope deferred makes the heart sick' (New International Version, Prov. 13.12)."

"Dum Spiro Spero", Latin for "While I breathe, I hope".

January 4, 1995

> "'He provides food for those who fear Him' (New
> International Version, Ps. 111.5)."

January 7, 1995   Following is an excerpt from my journal.
Behind on my bills; no money at all for food; and yesterday was pay
day. It's all gone. It is interesting to me that three days before, I read
that He provides food. I think it is curious that I never asked anyone
for food. I could have asked family or friends and I know they would
have been willing to help. Maybe pride, or maybe I felt I needed to be
punished for not taking better care of my finances. I really don't know.
I don't think it occurred to me to do so.

January 12, 1995   In the morning.
     "Lord, I know I should not worry about the fact that I am
behind on my bills, but it is hard not to worry. The alimony is late this
month. The electric company called because I owe them money. I am
trying to remember that you own everything, that your wealth is
unfathomable and that you have supplied in the past. Help me
remember, Lord."
     The verses that stuck out to me today are:

> "'Only be careful and watch yourselves closely so
> that you do not forget the things your eyes have
> seen' (New International Version, Deut. 4.9)."

God's provision in the past
     Absolutely a good rule to follow. We are so very short-sighted
as human beings. We usually look at what is going on in front of our
eyes, and forget that He is there, and He is aware. He is our "steady
place".

> ""'it's all right", he said. "Don't be afraid. Your God,
> the God of your father, has given you treasure in
> your sacks; I received your silver." Then he brought
> Simeon out to them' (New International Version,
> Gen 43.23)."

Seriously, when I came home from work today there was a check for $250.00 in the mail! Thank you, Lord. We shouldn't always look for an immediate answer, but just know an answer is on its way.

JANUARY 15, 1995   Today is Sunday and I didn't go to church. I have to keep wearing the same blue skirt and sweater because I've gained weight and can't fit in to anything else. That is not a good reason not to go to church; pride taking over. I'll go this evening when I feel more comfortable wearing jeans. Sometimes when depressed, we don't eat; sometimes we eat too much, or too often; or both.

"'Remember Your word to your servant, for You have given me hope' (New International Version, Ps. 119:49)."

APRIL 6, 1995   A big fight at my place between my children. Both little girls were crying. Everyone is so upset. "O Lord, help us!!!

JANUARY 1, 1996   Lord, I am beginning this year as distressed financially as last year at this time, and making less. I dare not compare where I am with where someone else is; not emotionally, financially or spiritually. When I do, I become angry, complacent, or prideful.

JANUARY 2, 1996   I saw how Satan got Eve's eyes off of all the good God gave her and set her sight on that one tree He told her not to eat. For me, he gets my eyes on my financial bondage, and hard family times, and off of the truth that He is here every morning and He will provide; He is aware of all circumstances, and He does not panic.

JANUARY 6, 1996   Yesterday I wrote a check out for my rent and I don't have the money in the bank. I took a second part time job at Gertrude Hawkes. I worked for them over Easter last year.
          In Genesis 22 I read today that rom God comes deliverance. But deliverance doesn't always come immediately. That, however doesn't change the fact that He, Himself, is present always. He is steadfast, steady, and wanting only good for us; His good, for our good.

201

JANUARY 7, 1996   Lord, you know where I am; deliver me
from this pit of discouragement, and put me where you want me.

FEBRUARY 2, 1996   This is what the Lord brought to my mind
this morning at the closing of my prayer time.

> "'But as it is written, eye hath not seen, nor ear
> heard, neither have entered into the heart of man,
> the things which God hath prepared for them that
> love him' (King James Version, 1 Cor. 2.9)."

FEBRUARY 8, 1996   The Lord said to me, "You will not die, I
have something for you to do." (I was concerned about dying because
I was about to have an operation) I've always wondered, and still do to
this day, what that "something is". Perhaps it is a series of
"somethings". Perhaps I'll never know. But He knows.

FEBRUARY 17, 1996

Muffled
I am crying, Lord,
I just can't seem to make a sound;
I am crying, Lord,
Though the tears aren't seen flowing down.

MARCH 26, 1996

Hidden Behind the Smile
Up, up they climb the ladder of success,
And as they smile,
All the while,
Hide pain behind their dress.

JANUARY 3, 1998   I am so tired.

JANUARY 8, 1998   I woke myself up humming tune to "How
Can I Give Thanks for the things You have done for Me". I hummed
whole song in my sleep. I mentioned this to the pastor and he said, "it

is because the Holy Spirit feels at home in you." I would have never thought of that.

JANUARY 9, 1998   Something the pastor said recently came to mind today. "We can't arrange and regulate life so that we are happy all year through."

MAY 1998   I was asked to write a poem for parents whose baby died. I never met the parents, but could imagine how they felt.

Jillian Rachel
Jillian Rachel
This is your name
Though you are gone
Our love, you remain.

Jillian Rachel
Tiny and sweet
Our little girl Jillian
Now peacefully sleeps.

Jillian Rachel
Our baby adored
Now cradled gently
In the arms of our Lord.

Dear little daughter
For a time we're apart
You were here for a moment
But forever in our hearts.

34
The Millennium

JANUARY 1, 2000   This past year has felt very dry. Most of the year I've been off my Zoloft, wanting to make sure it doesn't hinder my feelings. I do know I have constant feelings of sadness, and restlessness. The word that comes to my mind is "caged".

JANUARY 27, 2000   Last night I woke up with the name "Noah Cooke" on my mind. I don't know who he is, but I believe the Lord put his name there, so I prayed for him.

SEPTEMBER 30, 2001   Our pastor of Faith Baptist church resigned this month. I wrote the following poem as a tribute to him.

Pastor
He has been faithful to the body,
Both as shepherd and a friend;
A serious man, yet comical and creative;
A real Folgers blend.

Not given to perfection,
But with only an occasional flaw,
The kind of pastor that Harmony says,
"Is just like a second grandpa."

Charity said this morning,
"When he leaves, the church will fall apart"
Her feeling we share, though we all know,
The church is the Lord's and lives in our heart.

We know for church history,
Pastor has an affinity

That is understandable since he's part of the Trinity.
Oops! I mean he studied Divinity.

On fellowship Sunday,
He sometimes says "Amen" with a sigh
Then a sly little smile spreads across his face
As he thinks of the lunch, and pot pie!

Now this is one half of the team, a slice of the pie
The other side of the coin is the apple of his eye!
A woman of wisdom, her name is Judy
She's listed in Proverbs as faithful in duty.

"Honey it's time to diet,
Dear, you are looking so tired;
Let someone else do it for a change,
You are already too wired!

Come take a rest, put life on a shelf,
Come my Diegel Beagle, and just be yourself."

The years have gone by so fast,
The two have seen many a change,
Now in God's mind and loving way,
He is going to rearrange.

Pastor Chuck and Judy, Faith's mom and pop,
Like Maxwell coffee commercials,
You are good to the last drop!

For all time to come,
In our heart you'll abide
If we lose touch of you here,
We'll meet you on Heaven's side.

Not one of my better poems, but heartfelt still.

205

The next year we had a younger man fill in as pastor. He was an honorable man and a good teacher, but it was hard for some people to get use to the changes that were being made.

JANUARY 1, 2002

Changes in the Church
O Lord, it is so hard to be part of the changes
In the place where I come to meet you;
I count on the sameness, the order, the plainness
Of all of the old I once knew.

Gum now a'cracking,
And little shoes whacking,
Kicking the back of the pew;
People are talking
And babies are squawking
In the place where I feel close to You.

Music so snappy,
I know it sounds happy
With clapping and moving the shoe;
But inside I'm hissing
For sadly I'm missing
The sweetness of times I've spent here with You.

Lord, are You calling
Away from my bawling
To come and enjoy something new?
And Lord are you raising
Those hands that are praising
And blending the old with the new?

In my heart are you whispering,
"My child, I am listening
And lovingly sitting near you."
Yet, it seems strange,
And I want to complain,
I'm not sure I like this, Do You?

JANUARY 3, 2002   Today I feel mean. Day Care check hasn't come yet.

JANUARY 4, 2002   I am starting day off feeling stressed and angry. I am stressed because of the soreness I've felt in my upper chest for two weeks, and this morning I found out I am overdrawn at the bank.

JANUARY 7, 2002   Tomorrow I have an interview in Mechanicsburg for a job in the activity department at Messiah Village.

JANUARY 9, 2002   I heard the Lord say in my heart, "I will do a new thing. I will provide."

JANUARY 11, 2002   I have been having scary dreams for about two weeks. I dreamed tigers appeared in the yard of a house where my daughter, who is a teenager, and my son, of grade school are playing with other children. There were about 5 tigers. I was terrified for my children and kept calling for my daughter to come up the steps in to the house. She was the oldest, but she couldn't hear me.

I dreamed a dream within another dream that really frightened me. I was yelling for my mother, only nothing was coming out of my mouth loud enough to be heard. I took my blanket and went in to my parent's bedroom in Pleasureville, Pennsylvania. My dad woke up first and knew I had had a scary dream because he said he also had them. My mother woke up and made room for me beside her; then I felt safe, and woke up from my dreams.

JANUARY 16, 2002   I am extremely discouraged.

JANUARY 22, 2002   It occurred to me last night while lying in bed that the Lord is the only Person Who can handle my feelings of anger.

FEBRUARY 4, 2002   I won't know anything about Messiah Village until Wednesday. (Incidentally, I did get that job, and was also rehired at another time. I retired from Messiah Village in 2012). Tomorrow I am to help a friend's friend to clean. She has MS.

FEBRUARY 7, 2002   I dreamed a whole group was meeting in a large church sanctuary, with the exception of my ex-husband, who was not there yet. We were waiting for him. Then I saw him off in the distance and noticed him trying to find us by using his hands. He was almost totally blind. I called to him to come forward 10 more rows, and he did begin to walk toward us. Then I woke up.

FEBRUARY 16, 2002   I never thought I would get much from reading Leviticus, but this morning I woke up with this thought from the Lord: For months and months I lost all desire to clean or decorate since no one was around to notice, and I convinced myself that it wasn't important to God, anymore then to me, and anyway it was reasonably orderly.
But as I pondered this I realized that He does indeed care. He wanted cleanliness, beauty, and order in His own place, and thus He does care about mine. That encouraged me to do something about the way I was thinking, and get to work!

FEBRUARY 20, 2002   I wake up mornings, look forward to a cup of coffee, and then afterwards begin to feel depressed, and I don't know why. I just don't feel like I have much to look forward to. One good thing is that I decided to do a service for church once a month. I am taking part in the cantata in June. My daughter and I are doing the bulletin board for May.

MARCH 3, 2002   The Lord does not desire that I continually feel depressed. He desires my good. The enemy wants what is bad for me; he deceives.

JUNE 3, 2002

> "'And He said unto them, Come ye yourselves apart into a desert place, and rest a while' (Mark 6.31a)."

JUNE 10, 2002   How we think so often determines our actions. Healthy thinking will produce healthy actions.

"'Stimulate you to wholesome thinking' (New International Version, 2 Pet. 3.1)."

JUNE 12, 2002

"'He who conceals his sins does not prosper, but whoever confesses and renounces them finds mercy' (New International Version, Prov. 28:13)."

JUNE 13, 2002

"'A fool gives full vent to his anger, but a wise man keeps himself under control' (New International Version, Prov. 29:11)."

JUNE 14, 2002

"'God turned the curse into a blessing for you, because the Lord your God loves you' (New International Version, Deut. 23.5)."

JUNE 15, 2002

"'Speak up for those who cannot speak for themselves' (New International Version, Prov. 31.8)."

APRIL 2003   While working as an activity assistant I wrote the following poem as a tribute to our volunteers.

Volunteers
You come into our unit
Most often with a smile;
Ready, willing, and able,
To walk the extra mile.

You always treat us gently
With respect and kindness too;
And never do we feel alone

When we take a walk with you.

Gifts come in many sizes,
Different needs to fulfill;
Sometimes reading, sometimes talking,
Sometimes sitting by us still.

You help us at the bake sale,
In the shops on the floor;
You give of your talent,
And then you give some more.

35
Walking Out of the Desert

In 2004 I was living in Tennessee and while there I got together with some women for a Bible study and time of sharing. We talked of our love for chocolate and other such goodies in which we sometimes indulged too much. The following is a poem I wrote after realizing how beautiful sin appears to us, and yet because it is deceptive, only leaves us with unfavorable and sometimes disastrous consequences. We often miss out on the best because we are too eager to partake of the first thing that is offered us.

Candy
Open the box, remove the lid
I'm delicious to eat, and a lift I can give.
Hmm, so many choices, where do I begin?

There's chocolate and caramel, Nugget and pecan,
Vanilla cream and strawberry dream,
And toffee's right on my lap,
If I eat it real fast,
The calories won't last
And then I can take me a nap.

Oh phooey, oh poop, do I hear a voice?
Are you speaking to me, Lord?
Saying, I have a choice?
But the chocolate I need when I'm feeling down,
Who cares at the moment if I'm looking round?

And strawberry pink, it makes me feel "up",
While vanilla, and toffee match my coffee cup.
Let me give it some thought,
My mind's in a whirl,

It spins and it gazes on raspberry twirl.

The decision is made, the verdict is in,
I'll close up the box so I can be thin.
There is one at our table, where we sit to eat;
Whose commitment to women is genuinely sweet.

With compassion, He serves others in need,
Walking in gentleness as He quietly leads.

JULY 17, 2005

Unrecognized Grace
Every day in ways unknown
His grace He pours from out His throne;
And though it often goes unseen;
It flows on me in steady stream.

Do you remembering me mentioning way back in the late 1980s that our family was totally split apart and not talking with one another? Do you remember the dream I had which referenced "Malachi" 4.6? Well at some point in 2006 our family began spending time together once again. My former husband had now remarried a very nice woman, and wounds were beginning to heal. As time went on, they, as well as our children and their families, and I spent just about every holiday together in one or the other's home. This kind of thing does not always happen. I don't even understand how it happen with us. Only God knows.

APRIL 2008   I bought the first new car I had in about 13 years. (I still own that car today. It is now nine years old.)

MAY 2008   This is the month my son gets married. I was privileged to hold a rehearsal dinner for him and his fiancé. The wedding was beautiful, and one of the special parts was when he sang to his bride at the altar.
        Throughout the lives of both of my children I prayed for spouses of the Lord's choosing, for each of them.

SEPTEMBER 2008   I drove my new car which I appropriately named, Miss Versa, to Michigan to help my niece, by marriage, with her ministry to the Mexican migrant workers and families. After spending a week with her, I then drove to North Carolina and spent a week with my son and his wife. They kindly arranged three groups for me to share my poetry with. One was a group of men, and the topic was on "Hope". One was to a group of women where I shared the poem "Midnight Rose". For this group I printed out a copy of the poem for each of the women, and gave each of them a rose. We also had rose petal candies. I was very appreciative of the opportunities to share with each of them. The third group were those who attended a Wednesday night prayer meeting.

After this I drove to Florida to visit for a week with my brother and sister-in-law. We spent time each day sitting on their lovely back porch playing "Three Kings", a fun card game.

These trips were made before I had a GPS, and so it was quite an accomplishment to drive that distance and be using a map. Following my trip to Florida, I returned to North Carolina, and then back to Pennsylvania. Whew!,

FEBRUARY 12, 2009   About a month ago I began considering having an evening when I invite people from the apartment building to my apartment so we could get to know each other better. There was a total of eight apartments in the building, including my own.

I considered buying invitations, and then thought to myself, "Oh, maybe someone will give me some that they don't want". The next day, in the mail, I got a small package from a friend in Tennessee. Inside were two packs of blank note cards, and stamps! My friend had absolutely no idea I needed them! I am only able to believe this was the hand work of God! A couple of weeks later I wrote out the invitations and taped one on each door of the apartment building. On the Saturday I chose, I made chili, and dessert. One person came. He was very shy and uncomfortable. He did not eat anything. We sat and chatted, and that was the end of that. I invited the young man to go along with me to church any Sunday that suited him. He never accepted. To what purpose was the whole thing? I'm not really sure. It all seemed rather uneventful, with the exception of the fact that I saw God work on my behalf. He gave me His "stamp" of approval.

MARCH 3, 2009   My ex-husband suggested I write a book
about our life. He felt it would help other women.
I wasn't at all interested. As I sit here now and write, some eight years
later, I still don't know if anyone will be encouraged or challenged by
what I write. I hope so. I do know that at this point in time I am ready
to write my story. I am learning things about myself as I write. I am
seeing how close the Lord walks with me, and how he keeps me going
in the right direction, when I don't always sense His presence with me.
I am seeing the strength he gave me to walk through each day through
difficult years, and I am seeing answers to prayers.

MARCH 14, 2009   I praise You Lord that I can come to you; for
forgiveness of my sins, and for your instruction for my life. I praise you
Lord for the beauty you have created; for life.

MAY 6, 2009   I woke up while saying in my mind,

"'Thy word is a lamp unto my feet, and a light unto
my path' (King James Version, Ps 119.105)."

MAY 24, 2009   A couple of times last night I woke up from
a fearful dream, and each time I was singing the old hymn, "Jesus,
lover of my soul; let me to thy bosom fly."

SEPTEMBER 7, 2009   My father died; the only earthly father I will
ever have. The day before he died, he was still living on his own, doing
his own finances, and driving his own car. I can still see him sitting at
the table working in his checkbook, and being so frustrated because
he couldn't find a two-cent error! Two days previous he and I were at
a gas station, and I was showing him how to use his Giant card to get
credit for gas pumped. Later that day he said do me, "You helped me a
lot today Barbara, you really did." That, and "I love you" when I left to
go home were the last words he said to me. I feel very sad that I didn't
know he would no longer be among the living in two days. So many
things left unsaid. So many questions left with no one else to ask. I
miss him.
          Two nights later as I stood beside his bed in the hospital right
before he died he raised himself up and said, "help me Jesus, help
me"! I said, "He will, daddy". A few moments later the nursing staff

came in and began chest compressions. They were done for quite some time and then they asked me if they could stop, and I nodded yes.

OCTOBER 10, 2009   Woke up last night singing two hymns. "Jesus, Lover, of my soul", (which I was also singing in May), and "Time after Time", by John Peterson, I think.

NOVEMBER 7, 2009   I don't understand why I am singing in my sleep. Last night I had a dream where I was singing an old hymn that we sang in church when I was a teen. "'Are You Able' Said the Master"?

JANUARY 4, 2010   My daughter is experiencing pain again; the doctor thinks Crohn's Disease may be active. It is so hard seeing her in pain because I cannot do anything to make it stop.

JANUARY 14, 2010   My son has a ganglion cyst on his right wrist. He is a piano player, and also works with computers. If only I could protect my children from pain. Pain, somehow, has a purpose. God, our Father, does not always protect us from pain. Jesus suffered greatly.

JANUARY 15, 2010   CAT scan showed that my daughter has an abscess where her bowel was hooked up years ago after having 12 inches removed. This was inconclusive, and on the 23rd a second c-scan showed a large part of her bowel has active Chrones again.

APRIL 23, 2010   My daughter is in the emergency room. She had to have a pus-filled sac taken care of immediately; it was so painful for her!

APRIL 23, 2010   I had a dream where I was playing the piano, and everyone was singing, "I've Got A River Of Blood Flowing Down On Me". I'm wondering if this is in relation to my daughter's bowel being cleaned out.

JUNE 7, 2011

Never Too Late
When I was young, I feasted on laughter and tears;
Life lay ahead with many of years.
I had time to wait, and days so to plan,
The joys of my life I held in my hand.

Minutes have spread and birthed what I lived;
Moments long gone have life still to give.
Where once overflowed the years from the hours,
And gifts blossomed forth from seeds into flowers.

The garden of life still has moments to spare
And living remains, and is meant to be shared.

It would be lovely to share life with someone; I think.

MARCH 7, 2011   Another precious baby joined our family;
my first grandson. He is the son of my son and daughter-in-law. While
he was still inside the womb, he was called "Pogo". Below is a poem
that I wrote for him, pretending these might be the thoughts he was
thinking.

JANUARY 2011

Pogo's Journey
I was looking for a home,
One created just for me,
For I am just a little egg
Who will one day be a he.

I wanted to find my mom
Who was married to my dad;
The two of them were waiting
And praying for a little lad.

My mom would have a waddle
And feed me like moms do;
My dad would learn to swaddle me,
Because I'd be brand new.

They'd be a little older
And wiser so I've heard
I'd rest upon their shoulder
As they read to me God's word.

We would play and laugh and sing,
And I would learn the rules;
They'd teach me such important things
Like how to cook and use the tools.

My dad says I must learn to work,
And help the neighbors 'round,
While mom is baking cookies
He'll show me how to pavement pound.

For I must be responsible,
Whatever that word means;
It's right up there with truth and love,
And keeping my mind clean.

And so I kept on searching,
While they on bended knee
Were praying for a little boy
To join their family.

Then all of a sudden
There they were
My dad and my mom

It's him! And it's her!

I recognized the two of them
By the light in their hearts that I lit,
And I knew that my Daddy in heaven
Had found me a wonderful fit!

Three months later my first great-grandson was born, and
since then another great-grandson, as well as my first great-

granddaughter, and in this coming new year of 2018, we will all welcome another new little one!

In August of 2012 my son and daughter-in-law asked me to move to South Carolina and live with them. I was both pleased and surprised they wanted me to do that. I retired and moved the end of the month. I had a lovely room and was in the presence of my precious 15-month old grandson.

During the time I stayed in South Carolina I met and had lunch with one of my son's co-workers. I was given a bag of chips with my lunch, and because I did not want to eat them I offered them to my lunch partner for her children. She refused because she had two children, so one bag of chips just would not do.

As we were eating a man came from another table and said he did not want his chips and gave them to us.
Problem solved. Immediately this fun poem came to me.

SEPTEMBER 15, 2012   For Kathy

A Bag of Chips
Me thought it just a bag of chips
Placed upon my tray;
Would not grow upon my hips
So I tucked them fast away.

I offered them to my friend
To take with her to child;
"Oh no", said she, "I need two,
For one would drive them wild!"

Above us stood an unseen God,
Who knowing more than man,
Prepared a second bag of chips
To upon our table land!

For He is God of great and small,
And reveals as He is able,
To keep bagged chips from lips and hips,
And gift them on a table!

SEPTEMBER 6, 2012   I am so concerned about my son. He is so exhausted!

SEPTEMBER 20, 2012   Dr. put my son on Thyroid medicine immediately.

The months in South Carolina proved to be very difficult for a variety of reasons, and I came home after being there only three months. We were all in agreement that this was not working out the way we hoped it would. I was both heartbroken and relieved at the same time. I will never forget the look on my grandson's face as I waved goodbye that day. It absolutely broke my heart.

Before I went out the door, he started walking toward his bedroom where some of his toys were. He said, "Foofoo" coming?" My eyes still fill up with tears when I think of that moment. Of course, I'm sure he doesn't even remember that day. (Now it is 2017, and guess who I'm living with! Yes, that is right; my son, and daughter-in-law, and six-year-old grandson!) The Lord is so good to make possible second chances for his children.

During the time I was in South Carolina I attended a small church where my family went. I met so many nice people there, and very much enjoyed those Sunday mornings.

In October my son was ordained as a minister, and for a time was fill in pastor for this small group of believers. He is an excellent Bible teacher. It was my privilege to be in this service, and to sit under his teaching for a time, in South Carolina. His father was also present in South Carolina for his ordination, and the weekend. I am so glad the two of them had this time together, for none of us knew at this time that his dad would only live a couple more months. The Lord was so gracious to allow this time for the both of them.

DECEMBER, 2012   My ex-husband and friend, and my children's father suddenly died on December 11, one week before turning 72. It was a tremendous shock! His siblings, and our family were by his bedside singing as he slipped in to the presence of the Lord. My son held his dad's funeral service with grace and dignity, and then ended up temporarily in the hospital from the loss and shock. Several people who attended shared remembrances and testimonies. Below is a poem I wrote and shared. As I wrote it I imagined these might be the words he would say if he had been able.

Christmas in Heaven

Christmas in Heaven, that's where I'll be;
Walking and talking, my Savior and me.
The wife that I love, and my children so dear,
Soon will be starting another new year.

My daughter, my son, both of you grown,
One day we'll share this heavenly home.
I had to leave quickly your families that night;
The time a surprise, and fast was my flight.

Good-bye to you spouses, your children so sweet;
Good-bye till the time again we'll all meet.
Good-bye to the painters and friends through the
years,
Those I have taught, and those who were peers.

I've laid down my brushes, my buckets of paint,
I've traded them in for the crown of a saint.
Trials are done, temptations are past,
I've finished my course, and I'm home at last.

Brothers and sisters, from beginning to end,
It's important you know I'm here with my Friend.
Jesus, dear Jesus, My Savior is He;
He guided my journey, And was waiting for me.

Upon returning to my home in Pennsylvania in January of 2013 I began to regularly go to a Baptist church in the area. I had attended there before the move to South Carolina but because of working every other weekend, I never felt really connected. But now I was able to attend both morning and evening Sunday services, and prayer meeting. The following year I joined the choir, and soon felt very much a part of the people. I made some very good friends there whom I still get together with in 2017 even though an hour drive separates us.

God is always working. He works to our benefit if we are one of His children. How does one become a child of God? What exactly does that mean? It means coming to a point in our life when we understand that we are people who sin, and because a Holy God cannot be in the presence of sin, He sent Jesus, who is perfect, to die for each one individually. When we acknowledge that we need Jesus to save us; and ask Him to save us, He will do it! That was His whole purpose for dying for us. Think seriously about this, and make a decision.

In April of this year the Lord reminded me that He doesn't need me to manipulate a situation in order to get His work done. Working in people's lives is His job, not mine. Really, who am I to know what people need; He is the only one Who really knows. I don't even know what I need all the time!

Charles Stanley said "the Lord always knows what we need; we ask for what we sometimes think we need, and when we don't get it, it is because the Lord is the only one who knows what we truly need".

MAY 3, 2013   The name, Mildred Jeduka came to me in a dream. I prayed for God's will for her life. This year, 2017, I searched for her name in people search, and found no such person. Perhaps she is in another country; perhaps she hasn't yet been born; perhaps she died. Only God knows.

MAY 4, 2013   I heard this at our lady's spring luncheon; "If you continue to do what you are doing, you will continue to get what you are getting". Is there something in your life that you want to see changed, and yet it never seems to do so? Worth thinking about.

MAY 26, 2013   I pray for my grandson and my great-grandson's salvation, and that they will walk a path of righteousness; possibly together in a life's work. (they are each two-years old at this point, with only three months between them. I like to think of them as Jonathan and David of the Old Testament.)

JUNE 1, 2013   Be on the look-out my children for lonely people; some of the friendliest, and most out-going ones are the loneliest. I think I may have sadly missed the mark myself. You will see what I mean when you get to August 14.

JUNE 12, 2013   Today was the first lesson in a Beth Moore video Bible class. I am attending the class with my cousin, at her church. It is on the book of Esther. One thing Beth Moore said in the video is that the Lord has something planned for His kingdom and our destiny, during the course of this nine weeks of listening and participating. Have you ever read the book of Esther in the Bible? If not, give it a look. There is an arranged marriage, intrigue, and a plot to murder! You will also witness deception, courage, and how important being at the right place at the right time sometimes is.

JUNE 18, 2013   If you remember back in 1986 I wrote a poem about feeling as though I were in a desert. Again today, I have that feeling.

Familiar Spot
I'm back in the desert, Lord
In a dry and lonely land;
Little to eat, cracked and tired feet,
And seeing nothing but desert sand.

I've often tried to get out,
Climbed walls, or tried to lay low;
Kept quiet, or given a shout,
But still I am here,
And the journey is slow.

An example of how alive God's word is, is that later this morning I was reading Acts 13 where the Apostle Paul recounts the wandering of the people in the desert when they left Egypt. Next I read ' (King James Version, Ps. 63, and here is David in a dry and thirsty land. One thing to make note of is that in both instances, the Lord was with them while they were in the desert, and he fed them too.

JULY 18, 2013   I feel as though I have "spiritual constipation".

July 21, 2013   I pray for Adam, Lord, for early salvation. I pray that he will have a heart of love for your people, and know how to shepherd them. Adam did accept Jesus as his Savior when he was three, and Leeland, just this month at age six. Isn't that so, so wonderful!

     I pray for Leeland, Lord, that he will be a voice among your people

August 5, 2013   Below is a little bit of what you will encounter if you read the book of Esther in the Bible.

Esther
for such a time as this
We met them one by one
In the pages of the Book;
So come take a walk with me
As at each life we look.

Xerxes was the king
Who owned a signet ring;
And from one ruler to another
Power it did bring.

Xerxes had a wife,
Vashti, the royal queen,
And such a stir she caused
When refusing to be seen.

All was not a loss,
For seen was in God's eye;
He prepared a plan, He had a man,
His name was Mordecai,

Who introduced with purpose
A wise and lovely miss,
And in God's time he told her
She was born for a time such as this!
God never fails His people,
He watches as He plans,

And though unseen, you can be sure
He holds us in His hand.

The Jews, they were in danger
For the King oft buried his head;
And an evil man named Haman
Wished all the Jews were dead.

And so in all his cunning,
He obtained the signet ring,
And quickly set his plan in place
For destruction of the Jews to bring.

He whined and colored the truth,
And made his motive a lie;
His wife said "Build the gallows!"
For to hang poor Mordecai.

But...

God never fails His people
He watches as He plans,
And though unseen, you can be sure
Mordecai was in God's mighty hand.

Banquet number one;
The process begun.
Esther made her request;
"Please dear King, I ask of you;
Bring Haman along to feast number two".

By now Mordecai had been honored,
And Haman was in a snit!
He knew he was in trouble
When too near the queen he did sit.

The king was in a fury,
And ordered Haman to swing,
But one thing was missing as he hung in the air,

King Xerxes retrieved that ring!

Esther was given the mansion,
Mordecai, the man now in charge;
Yet still the queen's heart was heavy
For all her people, at large.

Once more she was given permission
To speak before the king;
This was the time, and God's purpose
Jewish freedom now to bring.

And, as always, God never fails His people, He ever extends
His hand, And though unseen, we can be sure, He always has a plan.

AUGUST 14, 2013   Today I read the poem on Esther. It was our
last Bible study. After the Bible study was over a young woman whom
I did not know came to me and said she believed the Lord wanted her
to write a book. She asked me if I would mentor her, and I agreed to,
though I had never mentored anyone and wasn't even sure what that
meant, nor did I know anything about writing a book. We made
arrangements to meet for lunch, which we were able to do once.
During that time we shared about our families, and talked of meeting
again. The sad thing is before our second time together, she took her
life. I had no idea something was troubling her. She had a husband and
two little girls. I feel very sad about this. I completely missed out on
any cues that led to her taking her life. That is so tragic.

AUGUST 19, 2013   Today I met with a family member at a park
for a picnic. We usually do this once a summer. We catch up with one
another about our families, and what is going on in our lives. We also
pray together. This particular time she shared how she felt led at times
to "sit in the balcony" while her family works on particular issues,
rather than giving her input. That night I couldn't sleep because the
words of this poem started weaving themselves around in my mind.

AUGUST 23, 2013

A View from The Balcony

I'm sitting in the balcony, Lord,
Where you have put me today;
Watching blood-bought people,
And the various parts they play.

Each person has a part to learn,
And practice we must do;
My part is to sit in the balcony
As long as you want me to.

The rehearsals are not easy,
The stage seems way too small;
Some members have a large part,
And some are stuck on stall.

At times I grow impatient,
I want to direct the show;
And then you gently remind me,
That I'm here so I can grow.

All of us have such strange names;
Like "Frightened", and "Selfish", and "Mad",
And "Proud", and "Jealous", and "Hurting",
"Controlling", and also "Sad".

Your Spirit shines upon us,
As we rehearse the lines on each page;
You keep me in the balcony
And them upon the stage.

Then something slowly happens,
As you direct the show;
Your Light illumines each of us,
And we begin to glow.

"Frightened" becomes "Brave";
"Selfish" is more "Giving";
"Mad" is now much "Softer" and happy to be living.

"Proud" is showing "Humility";
"Jealous" full of "Grace";
"Hurting" and "Sad" are "Reaching Out";
"Controlling" has "Trust" on her face.

And I am humbled and "Thankful" in heart,
For on each face I see,
The reason that You set me apart,
Was to teach all these lessons to me.

AUGUST 31, 2013   Today I fell after taking Zumba water
aerobics, and tore my left shoulder cup. Had therapy for a time; opted
out of having an operation.

SEPTEMBER 9, 2013

Be
Be a fountain, not a drain;
Be the freshness in the rain
Be the nourishment in the cup,
To the hungry, lift them up.

SEPTEMBER 15, 2013   Today I went to my cousins for a
demonstration, with my daughter. The nicest part of the day was to be
able to spend it with her. Afterwards we went to my daughter's house
for dinner and then a game of Scrabble, one of our favorite games!
She beat me by two points! We started playing Scrabble when she was
a teen. I won most games then; now she wins more than I do! We
don't get to spend a lot of time together but I always enjoy her
company whenever we get the chance.
          It is now the end of September and I went to look for a gift
for my son-in-law for his birthday in October. I knew he liked audio
books and I found one I was pretty sure he would enjoy. It was about
the 12 disciples. I started to think about them and this poem came to
mind.

SEPTEMBER 28, 2013

Twelve Ordinary Men
They were 12 men;
An odd and earthy crew;
Much like many today,
With issues not a few.

Different ages, none were sages,
Some were rather brash;
Mending nets, tracking debts,
And one selling out for cash.

Fishermen brothers, doubters, and more,
Zealot, betrayer; rich and poor;
Leaders, and feeders, and worriers too;
Brave, and enslaved to lives they well knew!

Some married, some not,
Some young, and some old;
Some mild, and some wild,
And some so very bold.

Going about in routine of each day,
When Someone appeared
Who was known as "The Way".

He called each one to follow His plan,
He had a mission, and He wanted each man.
He knew of each weakness;
Was aware of each plight;
In some He saw meekness,
And in some He saw fight!

He held out His hand,
And in His firm voice,
He called them to follow
And knew well their choice;

And so one-by-one
United with Him

Until one crept out,
Perhaps never in!

But

His plan was not thwarted,
Nor ever aborted;
His resolve not diminished
From start to its finish.

He set His eyes straight,
His men by His side;
From Him they got purpose,
For Him they each died.

His cross not the end
Though His mission completed;
His blood promised life;
Death, He defeated.

He gave of His all,
And laid in a grave;
Full power remained
To ransom and save.

Up He arose, and with the sound of His voice, said,
"I am the Way", now you make the choice.

SEPTEMBER 29, 2013   Today I joined the Cedar Hill Baptist choir. It is so wonderful to be part of this group of people who love music and are so much fun! I really needed this connection. Thank you Lord for this gift.

For You, For Me
Is there a burden you need to share?
Is your heart heavy, filled with despair?
Is there a sin you feel you must hide?
No one to trust, and walk by your side?

Is there a weakness you're scared to show?
Long to run away, but no place to go?
Feeling the need to wear a happy face,
And hiding within a life of disgrace?

We are His hands to lift one another;
We are His feet to walk where He leads.
We are His mouth to teach from His word;
"You are my servant", thus saith the Lord.

JANUARY 12, 2014   My son preached a message today, and in it
he said, "Be encouraged. God looks on us at the point of our salvation
and sees His work, our sanctification, already perfect, even as it is
being completed in us; and for what? So we can point to Him, and so
others can see Him." So encouraging.

In 2014, at the age of 74, I was diagnosed with Chrones
disease. It is a bit unusual for a person my age to get it, but obviously
not impossible. I think it is very curious that no one, in our family
background had this. My daughter was the first, when she was only
19. When I think of that, how can I even think to complain! She has
been through so much more. She has been brave, and determined to
do whatever is best for her to do.

I had 12 inches of my bowel removed, just as she had so
many years ago, and after a year of being on medicine I was able to go
off of it, and am doing quite well.

When we are little children we many times want someone to
cuddle with us at bedtime. There is something warm and assuring in
having someone near as we close our eyes and drift off to sleep. As
adults, especially if we have had a mate separate from us, or die, or if
other circumstances have attributed to us being alone when it is time
for bed, we still wish for someone to cuddle with.

The next poem was written because I still have a little
grandson, now six, who continues to want his daddy or mommy, or
me, if I'm babysitting him, to cuddle with him at bedtime. To him, a
cuddle means lying beside him talking over the events of the day,
counting the cars as they drive by, naming the books of the Bible,
singing, and/or praying.

As we grow older and we no longer count cars, nor
necessarily sing before falling asleep; we probably still desire someone

near us to talk over the events of the day, pray with us, and cuddle before drifting off to sleep. There is something comforting and reassuring in a cuddle.

JANUARY 31, 2014

Cuddle Time

When I lay down at night
And all is quiet 'round,
The things that flood my mind,
In daytime can't be found;

For I am busy, on the run;
My thoughts are occupied
With family, friends, and having fun,
Not closing up my eyes.

But now here in the quiet
With nighttime dark and long,
I sense I feel removed
From daytime's happy song.

Imagination runs amuck,
My feelings are a muddle,
And now I want some company
To sit with me and cuddle.

I lay and talk with God,
Review my busy day,
And ask Him to remove,
And keep my fears at bay.

And as I grow real tall,
And darkness has less fear,
I will then be comforted
By knowing He is near.

Yet, even then, I'll struggle
With deep things on my mind,

And sometimes I will lie awake
And wish that I could find

A quick release from sleeplessness
And cares of days a muddle
But I'll still desire and hope to find
Someone to share a cuddle.

FEBRUARY 9, 2014   Praise God; I stand on His Word, and the finished work of Jesus for my salvation; for my assurance. This same year I was asked by my church's missionary fellowship to write a poem for the luncheon. The speaker was a pastor's wife, and her topic was to be, "The Many Hats We Wear". For those of you with busy lives, I'm sure you understand the meaning of that topic.

APRIL, 2014

Hats
When I was just a newly born,
They plopped upon my head,
A tiny little bonnet
When I was laid in bed;

For to add some warmth,
And joy of looking sweet,
But little did they know
Without a hat, I would never feel complete!

This brings us now to the present day
And our time of "this and that",
But hold on for a moment, Until I get my hat!

Monday is here and on my list
Is laundry first, of course;
Then wash kid's hair, car pool, day care,
Buy oats for Grandpa's horse!

Tuesday is the day of prayer,
And the meeting is at my place;

We need a treat for "pray and eat";
The pressure is building, "Lord, give me grace!"

Clean and dust, remove that rust,
Buy litter for the cat;
Mend Sadie's dress, pick up the mess,
Stitch lace on Sunday hat.

Wednesday arrived, and the silence is golden!
Wait, there's a knock at the door!
It's the preacher and Lizzy, all in a tizzy;
No one showed up to collect for the poor!

"Can you do this? Can you do that?"
Keeps running 'round my head;
"Sure, I can, and I will",
As I looked for a hat, the one trimmed in red.

Thursday morn and I'm forlorn,
My hat fell in the soup;
The one to wear at Farmers Fair
While serving lunch with the group.

Friday is here, and I'm so relieved,
No bonnet is needed today.
Is that the phone? "Your tire went flat?
You just stay calm, I'm on my way.

No, it's no problem, I'll get right on it;
I'm halfway to the car;"
Run to the bank, fill up the tank,
And tie up quick bonnet!

It's Saturday, and I just remembered
The ladies need a covered dish
For noon times "chit and chat";
Its only nine, I have the time
To don another hat.
Now, where is that hat?

Where is it at?
The one that sits atop?
No time to comb, or sit at home,
And my updo is about to flop!

I must practice my solo,
Take Jr. to polo,
Make bread for communion table;
Phone call "Pap"
To wake him from nap'
And check out computer cable!

Ah, Sunday morning, the first day of the week;
We stand, and we sing,
We worship our King,
We bow low before His throne;
And so grateful in prayer,
With joy, I declare,
I left my Sunday hat at home!

Do these hats sound like any that you wear, or perhaps you
have a bit more balance in your schedule then this woman has.
Sometimes it is easier to keep "doing", than to practice "being", for we
have the mistaken idea that doing more actually gets more done; I
guess it depends on what is important to you to get done, or be. Think
about that.

April 18, 2015

The Gift Box Of Talents
In this box I have a gift
The Lord has given me;
It's wrapped up tight, kept very safe,
It's only one you see.

I really haven't opened it,
Just placed it on a shelf;
He gave to others two or three,
Guess this one is for myself.

See her sitting over there,
He actually gave her four!
But one, He only gave me one,
Only one, no more.

All the work will get done
Most of the needs are met;
I'll keep my gift prettily wrapped,
No need to open it yet.

Here He comes looking pleased,
And offering His "Well Done",
He walks up to me, And can very well see,
I've protected my only one.

He says, "Loose the ribbon, and lift up the lid",
As His eyes fill up to their brim;
Can you imagine the shock, as I look in my box,
And see the gift to be shared was Him?

If the Lord has given you only one gift it is enough for you to do the work He wants you to do. Have you given any thought to what gift(s) the Lord has given you to share? Someone needs the benefit of what He has given you.
This year when it was once again time for our ladies spring luncheon, I was so pleased to be asked to come up with something new to share. The Lord once again reminded me of Who He is, and these words followed.

Jesus
May I have your attention,
This is something rich to hear;
It's not a new invention,
But truth to bring you cheer.

We each experience trials
And tests along our way;
But the Shepherd King of glory
Is with us every day.

You've met Him I'm sure,
You've heard of His fame;
Faithful and True;
God is His name

He's the Tower you can run to,
Safe to abide;
The Rock you can cling to,
When strong is the tide;

He's the Light you can follow,
When dark seems the way;
The God Who so faithfully
Leads you each day.

You may not see Him;
His voice be unclear;
Still He is walking, faithfully near;

The God of all ages knows the lay of the land;
Jesus is faithfully holding your hand.

He walks with you down in the valley;
He walks with you through desert sand;
He's climbed every mountain before you,
And He never lets go of your hand.

These words became a song.

JUNE 22, 2016

"'When you go to war in your land against the enemy who oppresses you, then you shall sound an alarm with the trumpets, and you will be remembered before the Lord your God, and you will be saved from your enemies' (New King James Version, Num. 10:9."

Today when I read this I thought about how often I should have signaled for help during my life, and how often I didn't. I just wanted to fix things on my own, including myself. Are you like that too? Sometimes we don't want to involve others in our problems because they may suggest we change something that we are not ready to change. Some people may respond in a way that is not helpful to us; they may truly not understand, nor even be interested in coming to our aid. Sometimes we just don't want to give people a chance to help. Maybe we are too proud. Maybe it is too scary to depend on someone else. Perhaps we make ourselves too vulnerable if we open up to others, and ask for encouragement, advice, or whatever we may need. We sometimes choose instead to isolate ourselves and pretend that all is okay. This can become a pattern for defeat, and loneliness, and yes, even pride. Here in this chapter the Lord encourages Moses to "sound an alarm" when in trouble. Should we not do the same? There are times in our lives when we should blow the loudest trumpet available! Where's that trumpet, Lord?!

SEPTEMBER 15, 2016

It Takes Time
It takes time to grow a flower
From a tiny little seed;
It takes time to prune a garden
From every growing weed.

It takes agreement to allow
The digging of a root;
The pulling, tugging, grabbing hold
Of strong and stubborn shoot.

A fearlessness in fear,
Acceptance of the pain,
Desiring, desperate, if you will,
Of life cleansing in the rain.

We are not the Gardener
holds the spade and hoe;
Who desires to plant within us

All he wants to grow.

Fallow ground: uncultivated, and unseeded;
Waiting to be sown and grown.

Recently I heard a teacher use a gardener and gardening as a good example of how to grow good healthy crops. He talked about the need to cultivate, break up the fallow ground in order to prepare it for the soon to be planted seeds. I thought about the poem "Midnight Rose" that I wrote in 1985, where the Gardener (God) knows that with tender care each of us can become a rose. But we must be willing to allow Him to dig up the dirt, sometime in the form of lies we have fed ourselves. It can be easy to feed oneself with lies like, "I'm no good"; "It is impossible for me to change"; "Who really cares"? "I'm too old"; "I'm too young, too fat, too dumb", "too busy". The other side of the coin might sound like, "I know better"; "I don't need anyone's help"; "I'm smarter, wiser, bigger, stronger"; and on and on the lies go. I remember hearing my father say once, when he perceived someone ignored him, "that's okay, I don't need them". The fact is he really did need their recognition, but he was so hurt, it was easier to tell himself a lie then face the truth that he was hurt. I've used some of these lies myself, at times. Probably most of us have. It is of upmost importance that we recognize them as such, as soon as possible, and then tell ourselves the truth. We must be willing to allow the God who created us to pull up the roots of the lies, the despair, depression, and hopelessness that we are apt to cling to. And we must allow and accept the new seeds of truth that he wants to sow. We must be careful not to "vomit" up the truth because the "roots" that choke off life and dreams are easier to digest. He wants to grow us, to change us, and to give us new hope. He wants us to live in the truth. Him. The Truth.

This is seldom a quick easy process, but then God is never in a hurry.

"'Jesus said: "I am The Way, The Truth, and The Life.
No one comes to the Father except through Me'
(New King James Version, John 14.6a)."

This year, in September I received another invitation from my son and daughter-in-law to come live with them. I had in previous months asked the Lord if this might be a possibility in the future. I was periodically making hour trips to their place to babysit, and I thought it would be easier if I were with them, or at least closer to them. Also, my lease was to be up in January, at which time my rent was to go up again. It did appeal to me to have family around, but as before there were also the "what if's" in my mind. It is not an easy thing to move in with someone; family, or otherwise, when one has been independent for 30 years, even when love is there. I was, however, excited when they asked me, and it was decided that January 1 would be my move in day.

Since my lease was not officially up, it gave us plenty of time to complete the moving process in February.

Since I was having a dinner at my place the evening before the New Year for some of my closest friends, it was decided that I would make the move on January 1. I only wanted to take those things that were immediately necessary.

My chosen necessary things were clothes, a few books, my Bible, budget notebook, and pens. I also decided I needed my two-cup coffee pot to get me started in the morning, and my trusty fan to keep noises of the night out. There are many things in life I would enjoy having, but truly only very few that I consider extremely important. You just saw the list! If you made a list of what was most important to you, what would be on it?

Remember the phrase from Robert Burns' poem "To a Mouse": "the best laid schemes o' mice an' men gang aft a-gley" [1]? He said it in old English, I believe, but we say it in the language most of us understand: "The best laid plans of mice and men often go awry." This saying very much applied to what happened to me on January 1. I was not able to move, for a virus "made its move" into my throat.

JANUARY 1, 2017   Last night our group got together for dinner and games at my place. It was then that I told my dear friends that I would be moving in with my family. It was to be our last evening together, in my apartment, and in all probability, as a group. How I enjoyed being with these people! During the evening my voice started to sound just a little bit odd to me, but no one mentioned it, and I did not pay too much attention to it either. We were having such a good time. We closed the evening by standing in a circle and praying for one another, and then with hugs and leftovers my friends one at a time left.

When morning came I could not utter a sound; barely a whisper! The virus in my throat lasted for 14 days. I could neither talk nor whisper during that time. Moving day would have to be postponed. This was not going according to my plan! I was so disappointed, but for a while I appreciated the silence after coming off a very busy holiday time. After a few days I started to grow tired of the solitude and felt isolated from everyone because, in truth, I was. During the first week, I was reading in ' (King James Version, Prov. and a verse jumped off the page at me. I decided after reading it that it would be my verse for the new year. It was so applicable, and continues to be so when my plans, my thoughts, are changed, sometimes against my wishes.

JANUARY 4, 2017

> "'A man's heart plans his way, but the Lord directs his steps' (New King James Version, Prov. 16.9)."

JANUARY 9, 2017   I am sitting here having devotions and pondering the up and coming move to my son's. I am thinking of the unknowns and challenges, and my eyes fall on my drinking cup with a very familiar verse of scripture on it. (The cup was given to me by one of my dear friends from my former church.) The verse is so familiar that it is easy to overlook. This morning, however, it speaks to my heart.

> "'Trust in the Lord with all your heart, and lean not on your own understanding. In all your ways acknowledge Him, and He will direct your paths' (New King James Version, Prov. 3.5-6)."

The middle of January I made the move. The official move-out date at the apartment was the first weekend of February. Some very dear friends came and helped me pack up all the rest of my belongings. They helped to provide boxes, wrapping material, tape, and manpower, or perhaps I should say womanpower. They also took me out for lunch. These two ladies were such a help to me.

Another friend from church provided the truck, and my family provided the arms, legs and backs to help me move. When we got to my son's, the pastor and another gentleman from our soon to be new church were there at the house to help unload. How gracious of them.

My son and daughter-in-law gave me the biggest bedroom because they knew how much I like to sit and write. I did not want to take this room, but they insisted. That was a very kind and generous thing for them to do. It is in this room that I started my story in April, and it is in this room that I sit and write even at this moment.

They also told me I was free to entertain people just as I always had, and they have been true to their word.

I settled on a church in the area immediately. It was, of course, the one whose pastor was so ready to help on moving day. Other essentials I've put off. I am still using the same doctor, eye doctor, and hair dresser about an hour away from my new home. The process to make these changes is coming slower than it probably should. Just this week I made arrangements with a new dentist.

I frequently get together with friends from my previous church. They are all an hour away. I will admit leaving my church and my friends has been difficult. I am very glad I am able to make the drive several times a month to visit with them. They also have driven my way, and at times some of us meet half way in between. It does concern me a bit that the time may come when none of us are able to make the drive. I am blessed to have a couple of younger friends who may be willing to pitch in and help us all get together on occasion.

I am part of a new congregation now and the people are very nice. I've already had a number of them to our home for dinner and games. The pastor's sermons challenge me, and keep my attention, for my mind can easily wonder if there isn't something that grabs hold of and captures it.

FEBRUARY 21, 2017   What a wonderful, freeing thing to know that my sins were all forgiven at the cross! In March of this year my doctor said my liver enzymes were all out of whack. I had several blood tests and each one showed a small change that wasn't good. I began to lose my appetite which was very unusual for me, and I also started to feel a bit depressed. I thought perhaps I had a serious disease and I was scared. I remember lying in bed one night and saying to the Lord, "Well, this is where the rubber meets the road". I knew that I had to make a decision to trust Him, or not. I decided to trust Him to help me whatever the problem was. It is simple to write these words, but the action of trusting is not always as simple. I did make the decision to trust Him. The G.I. doctor finally figured out the problem came from taking too much of a cholesterol medicine, and as soon as he took me off of it my liver bounced back to normal.

Sometime during the last few years the Lord saw fit to bring me slowly out of the desert. At times I did not think I would survive the trip trudging through it. But He was always watching over me, and giving me the strength for each day. It is possible that I was largely responsible for being in the desert; I'm not sure. I can't say that I know how He looks at it, but I have never felt the sting of His disappointment. He has always been kind, loving, and given me the strength and resolve to go through it, and I can see my walking out as I look back over the years and I realize I am no longer there.

What about you? Are you in the desert? If so, look around for the food He has prepared, in order to give you strength. Ask Him for the water that will refresh you and enable you to keep going, even though at times you will be trudging through deep sand. You cannot make it through, and out without Him; and be sure to blow the trumpet loud enough so those who love you can hear it!
I am well fed, and watered by the Holy Spirit of God. The Lord is more faithful to me than I am to Him, for I too often allow this business of life to short-change Him. He is able to handle everything because He is the "Cup" that never runs dry.

NOVEMBER 11, 2004   Written 13 years ago

Petals
Tiny, little petals
Wrapped around real tight;
Brown and frayed from scary storms
That come in darkest night.

Tiny, little petals
Build a fortress strong;
Wide and deep and thorny
To protect inside the song.
Within those soldier petals

Guarded from life's blight,
Grows a lovely shaded bud,
Desirous of the light.

Remove yourselves oh guardians,
For truth now surely grows,
And slowly, sweetly, quietly,
Comes the birthing of a rose.

36
Being Taught by the Master

Here at my son's I am learning lessons. I remember telling a friend from my previous church, as well as my pastor, that I knew there would be things the Lord wanted to teach me through this move. I didn't know specifically what they would be, but I've lived long enough to know we are always in the process of learning, or at least it is wise to be open to all the Lord desires to teach us. Here are some of the things I've learned about myself, and ways the Lord is trying to continue to "grow" me. It is said in another way by Jesus in the book of John.

> "'I am the true vine, and my Father is the husbandman. Every branch in me that beareth not fruit He taketh away: and every branch that beareth fruit, He purgeth it, that it may bring forth more fruit. Now ye are clean through the word which I have spoken unto you.' (New King James Version, John 15.1-3)."

He wants to prune each of us, and that is a very good and loving thing.

Lesson 1

I've learned I can sometimes be inwardly judgmental. When you live alone for 30 plus years and you only have yourself to consider, it can be difficult to bend to someone else's way of doing things. Sometimes this is why we hear people say, "She (he) is so set in their ways." Many times that is exactly what happens. When I have a critical thought, the Holy Spirit helps me to recognize it immediately, and I am thankful for that. I can then confess it, and ask the Lord to help me with this attitude. He is doing that.

Lesson 2

Another lesson the Lord is teaching me is that though I am intuitive, I do not always see things correctly. This reminds me of the first part of one of the poems you read earlier in this book. It reads like this:

Unseen
I only thought I saw,
But what I saw was not
The thing I should have seen,
The thing I should have got!

I am learning that I sometimes make incorrect judgments about what people say or do. I think I know their motives. I must be very careful of this. The Lord has shown me on more than one occasion that I have made an incorrect assessment of someone's intentions. Intuition, or discernment must always be under the Holy Spirits direction. It is a good gift and must be carefully used.

Lesson 3

I am more aware of how much I like to govern my own time. This has become extremely obvious to me since I started writing this book. I get lost in what I am writing, and I have little desire to come out of my room, even to do the things I most like, and to be with the people I love. When you live alone you can pretty much control your time, but with others around you need to be careful of being too selfish with your time, and isolate. My six-year-old grandson doesn't believe in isolation, of any kind, for any amount of time! I have to set limits for his visits to my room, and I do, but I still need to be considerate and open my door for my six-year-old visitor. As I read back over this paragraph I am aware how the Lord is able to use anyone of any age, in any condition, and in any walk in life, to help teach someone else a lesson they need to learn. No person is too young, or too old to be used of the Lord. Can you see the worth each one of us has in God's eyes?

Lesson 4

I am learning I can be defensive at times. I feel a strong need to protect myself, and avoid criticism. I have found that sometimes I am defensive when there really is no need to be. This is another lesson the Lord is teaching me.

Lesson 5

I can do nothing without the Lord. I am not good without the Lord. I cannot change myself; I can only change by the power of Almighty God within me. These statements are becoming increasingly real to me. These are not just words that I am saying because I've heard them said by preachers. These are statements I am making because I know them to be true.

It seems to me that five lessons at one time are enough for me to handle. Thus far, these are the ones I am aware of. He may have a different idea, and it is possible number six is not far behind. Some lessons take a life time to learn, and then sometimes, it only seems that way, and we can "wake up" and realize that as he is walking with us, He has been changing us more into His image all along the way.

37
My Closing Desire

As I am sitting today in the "Salt House" of some good friends, and drawing to a close this chapter of my life, I find that my desire is for people to see how good God is; how full of creative power He is; how wise and purposeful He is, and to experience His love; to truly know Him. I desire that you, who are in the desert, even as you read, keep in mind that Jesus is wanting to walk with you. I want to encourage you. He will bring you out.

My desire for myself is to know His love deep in my heart. He has proven it over, and over, and over again.

"'For God so loved the world that He gave His Only Begotten Son that whosoever believeth in Him should not perish but have everlasting life' (King James Version, John 3.16)."

Cords of Love
Lord, You found me at Your mercy,
Where I stood in deep despair;
And you bound me with the cords of Love,
As Your Spirit met me there

Index of Poetry and Song

Works Cited

(1) Burns, Robert. "To a Mouse, on Turning Her Up in Her Nest With the Plough", November, 1785. www.rbwf.org.uk/to-a-mouse-on-turning-her-up-in-her-nest-with-the-plough-november-1785/

(2) "Walk." Merriam-Webster.com. 2018. www.merriam-webster.com (18 June 2018).

(3) Patrick, Melody. "Noise of Boys."

(3) "Walks." Thesaurus.com. 2018. www.thesaurus.com (18 June 2018) .

(4) Van Dyke, Henry.

(5) Zarfoss-Coldren, Dorothy. "I Cannot Doubt Him."

Made in the USA
Middletown, DE
07 July 2021